The fullness of Christ

The fullness of Christ

Ajith Fernando

with Sheila Jacobs

LONDON ● COLORADO SPRINGS ● HYDERABAD

Author's Note

I was somewhat reluctant to have my talks at the 2006 Keswick Convention published with minimal editing. When I told that to a University student on a campus where I was ministering, he responded: 'But that will be great, because the book will have the freshness that was there during delivery which does not usually remain when books are written.' I hope that this book will introduce Ephesians 1 to its readers in a fresh way.

I am grateful to Sheila Jacobs who has prepared an excellent study guide alongside my material. I trust this book will be an example of East-West collaboration, within the church, that shows that differences in culture can help enrich the church rather than cause clashes within it.

Contents

THE AIM OF THIS STUDY GUIDE

In this study guide, Ajith Fernando unpacks the first chapter of Ephesians, with its emphasis on the fullness of Christ that we enjoy as Christians. This book is designed to help you to get the most out of this first chapter and to provide keys to explore the rest of the book of Ephesians.

The questions in each chapter help relate the principles explained in the commentary to our own lives and situations. You can use this guide either for your own devotional time with God or as a part of a group. Enjoy your study.

USING THIS BOOK FOR PERSONAL STUDY

Begin by praying and reading through the passage and commentary a number of times before looking at the questions.

You may find it helpful to note down your answers to the questions and any other thoughts you may have. Putting pen to paper will help you think through the issues and how they specifically apply to your own situation. It will also be encouraging to look back over all that God has been teaching you.

Talk about what you're learning with a friend. Pray together that you'll be able to apply all these new lessons to your life.

USING THIS BOOK IN A SMALL GROUP: FOR GROUP LEADERS

In preparation for the study, pray and read the passage of Scripture and commentary over a number of times. Use other resource material such as a Bible dictionary or atlas if they would be helpful. Before each session, look through the specific materials you need for that study – see the chapter breakdown below.

At the top of each chapter we have stated the aim – this is the heart of the passage and the truth you want your group to take away with them. With this in mind, decide which questions and activities you should spend most time on. Add questions that would be helpful to your group or particular church situation.

Before people come, encourage them to read the passage and commentary that you will be studying each week.

Make sure you leave time at the end of the study for people to 'Reflect and Respond' so they are able to apply what they are learning to their own situation.

Make sure you always have pens and paper handy.

SPECIFIC ISSUES RAISED IN PARTICULAR CHAPTERS

Chapter 1
- You may like to have Harry Blamires's book to hand for this session.
- Provide an A4 exercise book for the group to use as their journal.

Chapter 5
- This chapter suggests that group members should have people to whom they can be accountable – as group leader, you might want to offer to be that person or to put people in touch with someone suitable.

Chapter 6
- This session may bring up painful feelings regarding fathers, fatherhood or adoption.

Chapter 7
- Provide a worship CD for the reflective time.

Chapter 8
- Make sure you have to hand a woman's magazine or newspaper which features star signs or articles about

New Age beliefs, spiritualism, reiki, alternative therapies and so on. Most newspapers and magazines feature astrology and there are often tarot lines etc. advertised, even in local newspapers.

- Before the session, you might like to do some research to get names of Christian writers, novelists and actors etc. You may need to ask for information at your local Christian book shop or through other contacts.
- Provide resources such as information about the work of the Jubilee Campaign, Open Doors etc. There might be a specific organisation your own church supports.
- Jubilee Campaign can be contacted at 96 High Street, Guildford, GU1 3HE or www.jubileecampaign.co.uk
- Open Doors can be contacted at Open Doors UK, PO Box 6, Witney, Oxon OX29 6WG or www.opendoorsuk.org.uk

Chapter 9
- You might like to find a magazine which has the outline of a popular soap opera plot. One of the weekend national newspaper inserts would be best as they often have a 'what happened last week' round-up. If your group does not watch soaps, think of a film or a book which has been seen or read by the majority of the group and use that as an example instead.
- Provide items for collage mentioned in the reflection time: magazines, card, paper, scissors, felt-tip pens and so on.

Chapter 10
- Words of a song/music might be needed for the reflection time.

Chapter 11
- Be aware that this session might raise tricky issues; for example, when the group thinks about a Christian they do

not like or if there are any who find it hard to share when faced with the question about being a 'private person'. Further difficult issues might arise when talking about whether your fellowship is a 'performance-related church'.

- You might like to provide some of the materials that have been suggested to help in prayer, or demonstrate what could be achieved.

Chapter 12
- Gather together some small stones or rocks, enough for each person in the group. Make sure the stones are flat enough to write a word on. Supply paint or felt-tip pens.
- During the reflection time, you may find out that there are people who are going through particularly bad times. Be aware they may need extra help or prayer.

Chapter 13
- Before the session, find suitable pictures of people from history such as dictators and those involved in genocide; murderers, terrorists or rapists who have made the news to show the group. Also, make or supply a cross, a wooden one or a necklace or even a cross made from cardboard.

Chapter 15
- People may need counselling or one-to-one prayer over issues that stem from their pre-Christian days. Can those options be available to them?
- Be aware that issues regarding 'calling' may need further chat and prayer.

CHAPTER 1

Sound teaching, good living

Aim: To understand the importance of grasping what we believe.

FOCUS ON THE THEME
Some of us were brought up as Christians, in loving Christian homes. But many people turn to Christ in later years. Spend some time sharing your testimony with others in the group.

Read: Ephesians 1:1,2,17
Key verse: Ephesians 1:17

When I was a child, my father used to get the annual compendium of talks from Keswick Week and my brothers and I used to read those Bible expositions. It is now a real joy for me to be doing some of those expositions. I'll be doing only chapter 1 but the committee said it might be good to start with a little overview of the whole book of Ephesians, so let me say something about the background of this book.

It was probably written when Paul was in prison in Rome, about six or seven years after he had done his ministry in Ephesus. That ministry had involved a lot of encounter with 'magic' and the occult. You might remember that evil spirits came out from the seven sons of Sceva (Acts 19). They tried to cast out demons by the name of Christ and they were punished for it. People burnt books on magic after they became Christians, and there was a lot of spiritual warfare in Ephesus when the gospel first went there. And in this book Paul seems to suggest that people still feared false spirits. They were still encountering some of these spiritual powers, maybe even going to them for help. Paul has to respond to this. I think this is something that all of us will face, with spiritual forces becoming as powerful and prominent as they are today.

● *What evidence do we have in society today that occult spiritual forces are getting more powerful and prominent?*

TEMPTED TO GO BACK

I know of a family where the husband is a drug addict. His wife is a devoted Christian today; amidst all her pain, she has somehow come through. But early in her walk with Christ, the leaders in her church were shocked to find out that she had gone to a soothsayer to discover why her husband had gone back to drugs. Young Christians sometimes are tempted to go back to these forces because they give quick results – unlike our prayers, which sometimes may take a little time to be answered.

Paul talks about the supremacy of Christ in Ephesians: how to engage in spiritual warfare, how these forces are going to be defeated and how the death, the resurrection and the exaltation of Christ has put him above these forces and how they will one day be completely defeated by Christ.

● *Sometimes it seems as if our prayers are like letters that have 'got lost in the post'. How difficult is it to keep persevering in prayer when God seems silent? Spend some time considering how great God is and how much he has done for us. How can you encourage faith within your group?*

● *Do you know any Christians who are young in the faith who need encouragement – and mentoring?*

That's one aspect of the background of Ephesians; another seems to be that they were grappling with the sins that they committed before their conversion. Paul talks about sexual purity, lying, stealing and things like that. This is very common in the Bible – Isaiah said that he was a man of unclean lips, living among a people of unclean lips; the sins of the people had become part of his own life. In Corinth, where sexual sin was very prominent, we find strong statements about sexual sin. There was sexual sin within the church and there is specific teaching on some of the sins that were found in the society and in the church as well.

ENCOURAGED TO GO ON

There also seems to have been some tensions within the church, probably between Greek-speaking people and the Jewish people. So we find strong statements on how Christ broke the barriers that separated people. There is a very high emphasis on the church: everything that is done in Ephesians is done within the context of the church, the body of Christ.

Against this background, we find Paul giving very specific teaching on how Christians are to behave, and this is the main thrust of chapters 4 to 6. There we find things about purity, about lying, about how to relate to different groups of people – children, parents, husbands, wives, employees, employers; how to battle the forces of evil that we encounter as we go through life.

- *Role-play one or two of the following scenarios in the light of Paul's teaching in Ephesians 5:22 – 6:9:*
  - *A Christian husband wants to go on holiday abroad but his wife is afraid to travel by plane*
  - *Thirteen-year-old Anna feels resentful because her dad makes her go to church every week when she wants to go shopping with her friends*
  - *An employer finds his employee has been stealing from petty cash but he knows the woman is a single parent*
  - *An employer asks you to do something that is against your conscience – but you've only just started the job and don't want to upset him*
- *How easy is it to make all our decisions according to Paul's teaching?*
- *How difficult is it to maintain moral purity today? Does it mean you should not watch certain films or read certain material? Where do you draw the line – swearing, sex scenes? Or does moral purity have a much deeper meaning regarding our inner life? Discuss.*
- *Is there any such thing as a 'little white lie'?*

Paul gives specific instructions on several practical issues that the Ephesians faced. If Christian leaders don't do that, then the behaviour of those who become Christians is going to be unchanged. We have found that very often Christians will act the same way that their parents acted towards their husbands or wives. Sometimes they even find themselves doing the same things that they disliked their parents doing. We were shocked to find out that a Sri Lankan pastor once said, 'You know, my wife doesn't get involved much in ministry and so I hit her, and got her to be involved.' The Christian leader to whom he said this had to tell him, 'This is not part of Christianity.' Unless they are specifically told that it is wrong, people might carry on doing things that were part of their life before, as if they were doing something Christian. So Paul gives specific teaching on family life, on relationships at work and things like that. He talks about lying; because when everybody in society lies, Christians are tempted to lie as well.

● *What might people think is acceptable 'Christian' behaviour if they aren't told differently? Is there anything that might be hindering your own Christian walk that you aren't sure about?*

But this specific practical teaching in Ephesians is backed by solid theology. The first three chapters of Ephesians talk about a theology that is going to undergird our lives and out of which is going to come the Christian behaviour covered in chapters 4–6. Kent Hughes describes the movement from theology to practice in Ephesians like this: 'From doctrine to duty. From creed to conduct. From word to walk. From exposition to exaltation. From the indicative to the imperative.'[1]

That's the way Paul moves. In chapter 4:1, he starts with the word 'therefore': 'Since we have this theology, therefore let us live in this way.' That's something he does very often in his Epistles. In Romans chapters 1 to 11 he teaches about theology and then chapters 12 to 16 talks about practical living. He starts Romans chapter 12 with 'therefore.' Galatians 5:3 also has the word 'therefore' and then leads on to the practical side, as does Colossians 3:5.

INFLUENCED TO ACT

All our studies are going to come from the theology section. Teaching theology today is a challenge because people have lost the sense of the importance of objective truth and therefore there is a heavy focus on the experiential side of Christianity. This is good; Christianity is an experiential religion and that's something we must never forget – but without a theological foundation, we won't have the strength to practise Christian behaviour. If our worldview is not influenced by Christianity, when we are under temptation and we face the force of its attraction, we could give in to sin.

● *'We don't need study groups in our church. We just love people, give them cups of tea and cakes when they visit, show them the love of Jesus, that sort of thing.' How would you answer someone who said this?*

During this trip to the UK, on the plane I was reading a book written by Lindsay Brown, the general secretary of the International Fellowship of Evangelical Students (IFES).[2] It's about university students and the tremendous impact they have had on the world. He talks about how he was chatting to an IFES staff worker from a country that had just elected their first evangelical president. Lindsay Brown told this staff worker, 'How wonderful it is for you to have an evangelical president.' The reply he got was very surprising. The staff worker said, 'It's a tragedy. He does not have a Christian mind.' Therefore corruption continues; he appoints relatives to positions of influence and power and his appointment is a scandal for the gospel. This man had had a Christian experience and testified to God doing things in his life but when it came to the practice of politics, he was not very Christian.

● *What might help you have a more Christian mind?*

Ephesians beautifully combines theology and practice and it tells how people can have theology that drives them to behave in a Christian way. Paul has a three-fold strategy in this book: firstly, he gives a theological basis. This is the basis from which he exhorts the people and he does it beautifully, meditatively and devotionally. He gives the theology devotionally, lingering with the truths of the gospel, repeating them, going deeper and deeper to delve into the riches of what Christ has done for us. Five times in this book he talks about riches and four times about the inheritance that we have. Then he gives practical exhortations on how to live the Christian life. And thirdly, he presents all this within the context of the community, the body of Christ. We put Christianity into practice not alone but as a community. Theology, exhortation and community life: these are the keys to developing mature Christians who practise Christianity in their life.

FURTHER STUDY

Read through the whole of Ephesians, noticing how the theology underpins the practical teaching. What can we learn from Paul's life about his approach to theology and its practical outworking?

Get hold of a copy of Harry Blamires's book *The Christian Mind: how should a Christian think?*[3] and study it.

REFLECTION AND RESPONSE

- Remember the testimonies you shared at the start of this study. How much has your life changed since you came to know Christ? What areas do you struggle with?

- If someone asked you to give a good theological reason for your faith, would you be able to? If not, how can you rectify this?

- How does what you believe affect what you do and say? Do your words and actions reveal your underlying faith in Jesus – or not?

In twos, think and pray about these issues. This week, keep in touch with at least one other member of the group by email, text or phone, to encourage them.

- Keep a group journal as you study Ephesians 1, noting week by week how, amongst other things, the theology of Paul's teaching is affecting your daily Christian lives.

CHAPTER 2

Authority and identity

Aim: To see the importance of believing the authority of God's Word, as we learn about our identity in Christ

FOCUS ON THE THEME
Imagine someone in a position of authority has told a very big lie. Make up some 'Stop press: Headline news.' about it. Afterwards, ask: How easy would it be to trust anything else that person said?

Read: Ephesians 1:1,2,17
Key verse: Ephesians 1:1

THE AUTHOR

Ephesians starts by saying 'Paul, an apostle of Jesus Christ by the will of God.' I'm going to share some things now that are usually given in a theological college and I'm doing it with a certain amount of fear. Today there are some serious challenges to biblical authority and people are not taking the facts of Scripture seriously and, because of that, there's a lowering of our sense of the importance of what the Bible says. So I am taking the risk of giving you some background truths about Paul as the author, because recently the authorship of Ephesians has been questioned.

Ephesians claims to have been written by Paul but some commentators are saying it was probably not, because there are differences between this epistle and some of the other epistles of Paul. There are forty-one words that are used only in Ephesians in the New Testament and there are eighty-four words that are not found in Paul's other writings, though they are found elsewhere in the New Testament. So the language is a little different.

Also there is a character to Ephesians that is not typical of Paul's epistles. Paul usually gives a lot of personal details. He mentions about thirty-five people in the last chapter of Romans, for instance, with a lot of personal details but that is not true of Ephesians. Some scholars say that it was probably written by an admirer of Paul, either soon after or some time later than the time of Paul. These writings are called 'pseudonymous writings.' A lot of good scholars have ably answered this question and the one that I have depended on most is Peter O'Brien, who has written a very good commentary on Ephesians.[4]

In defence of the authorship of Paul, let me say firstly that the book unequivocally, unambiguously claims that Paul wrote it. Chapter 1:1 says 'Paul, an apostle of Christ Jesus by the will of God'; while chapter 3:1 says, 'For this reason I, Paul, the prisoner of Christ Jesus for the sake of you Gentiles . . .' Four times the writer claims to be a prisoner (3:1,13; 4:1; 6:20) and that is a very strong point because it's so unambiguous. If this is not Paul writing, there's clearly a deception here.

Secondly, the uniform testimony of the early church was that Paul wrote Ephesians. Evidence from the second century and maybe even from the late first century shows that they accepted that Paul wrote this. People at that time were much closer to the events than we are and so we can expect them to be a little more accurate about their conclusions than we are; they were careful about weighing and evaluating their founding documents: and this is the third point that I want to make. Authorship was important in the early church. Some people say it's not a big deal –

this was a type of writing that was common in those days. However, a chorus of very respectable scholars points out that the early church believed that their authoritative writings needed to be from the writer who claimed to have written them. Pseudonymity was considered fundamentally deceptive in the early church, say these scholars. Eusebius, who is known as the father of church history, quotes Serapion, bishop of Antioch, who died in 211AD, as saying 'For we, brethren, receive both Peter and the other Apostles as Christ: but we reject intelligently the writings falsely ascribed to them, knowing that such were not handed down to us.'[5]

And the early church Father, Tertullian, who died around 215-220AD, referred to a bishop who was defrocked because he wrote a book called *The Acts of Paul and Thecla* and claimed that it was written by Paul.[6]

Well-known British scholar, Stanley Porter, says that 'the general, if not invariable, pattern was that if a work was known to be pseudonymous, it was excluded from any group of authoritative writings.'[7] Another scholar, Earl Ellis, said: 'Such writing was a tainted enterprise from the very start and could not avoid the odour of forgery throughout the history of the early church.' The early church believed that it was important that they knew who wrote their founding documents.

It is true Ephesians is not as personal as the other letters of Paul, yet it has many similarities with Colossians, and if Paul wrote Colossians, then it's quite clear that the same person wrote Ephesians. The lack of many personal references and the difference in style is probably because Ephesians, unlike the other letters, was written to a more general audience. It was probably written to a network of house churches in Ephesus and that region. It was a circular letter and so would not have as many personal details as his other letters.

Does it really matter? I think it does, because the battle is on for taking objective truth seriously.

● *'The early church believed that it was important that they knew who wrote their founding documents.' Why was it so important for them – and for us?*

THE MESSAGE

The Bible contains a message which goes against what most people do and think today. It has absolute rules of morality which people consider quite outdated. There is a proclamation of the absolute uniqueness of Christ; he is One who is not like any other and people will look to various ways to reduce the claims that Christianity makes. I think this is why books like *The Da Vinci Code* have become so popular, because they deny some of the absolute statements that the New Testament makes. If what Ephesians says about its author is not true, how do we know that other statements that it makes, which are absolutely binding for our lives, are true? Why not rather take this as an inspiring book, instead as an inerrant guide for our daily life? If it is truly the word of God, it should be absolutely binding and we must take it as authority. Therefore we cannot drop statements that it unambiguously claims as being important.

● *'The Bible's got some good moral teaching but I don't agree with all of it.' How would you answer someone who has this pick'n'mix idea of belief?*
● *Many people found* The Da Vinci Code *intriguing and perhaps even believable, although it is a work of fiction. Why do you think people are so interested in books or films which seek to challenge the truth of the gospel and the authority of Scripture?*

The letter starts with the words 'Paul, an apostle . . .' The word 'apostle' was considered in the New Testament to refer to someone who was specifically commissioned by Christ. Apostles were important people. Paul was establishing his credentials; drawing attention to the official character of the letter. He says he's an apostle of Christ: not by his own choosing but 'by the will of God' (Eph. 1:1). Therefore what he is saying is important because it comes from an apostle.

Then he talks about the people who are going to receive this letter. 'To the saints who are in Ephesus and are faithful in Christ Jesus . . .' This one little statement contains four important things about Christians.

Who they were

They were 'saints'. The word 'saints' appears in six of the salutations of Paul's epistles – obviously it's very important. It means 'set apart' or 'holy.' We belong to God. 1 Corinthians 6:19–20 says '. . . do you not know that your body is the temple of the Holy Spirit within you, whom you have from God? You are not your own . . . you were bought with a price. So glorify God in your body.' Saints are people who have been set apart for God.

This means that things that displease God can't be in our life; that's what Paul is saying in that passage from 1 Corinthians. He says, 'You are not your own.' The passage is talking specifically about sexual immorality, but anything that displeases God cannot be part of our lives.

A mother visited her son in the university and went to his room and found twelve rather suggestive pictures of women in various stages of undress. She got a shock but did not say anything. She went home and sent the son in the post a beautifully framed picture of the head of Christ. This boy was thrilled by the picture and put it just in front of his desk. That night, before he went to sleep, he felt a bit odd about the combination of pictures in his room. So he took the picture that was closest to the head of Christ down. Little by little, he took down all the pictures, because he knew that they couldn't remain in the room along with the head of Christ.

Being a saint also means that we live only for God. Florence Nightingale, one of the great British women, only began her training as a nurse when she was thirty years old. She wrote this in her diary: 'I am thirty years of age, the age when Christ began his mission. Now no more childish things. No more vain things. Now, Lord, let me think only of Thy will.' A holy person lives for God only. When she was near the end of her career, someone asked her what her life's secret was, and this is what she said: 'I can give only one explanation . . . I have kept nothing back from God.' She was totally devoted to Christ.

A saint is also one who glorifies God in their bodies, as 1 Corinthians 6:20 says. We reflect God's nature because we are like God. A child was asked, 'Who is a saint?' He remembered all those stained glass windows with saints in his church and said, 'A saint is one through whom light shines.' The light would come into his church through the windows with the saints, and he had unknowingly given a beautiful definition of a saint.

● *Saints are 'set apart' or 'holy' – but we live in the modern age. How can we live 'set apart' lives that honour God (a) at work (b) in our times of recreation (c) in the way we live our daily lives?*

● *What does it mean to 'glorify God in our bodies'? Might it mean different things for different people?*

Where they were

Secondly, they were 'in Ephesus.' That tells us that Christians have an earthly address. We live for God only but we do so on earth. There's some question whether these words 'in Ephesus' were part of the original letter but if it's there, it points to our dual citizenship. We are sent by God into the world. William Barclay says that every Christian has a human address and a divine address. Separation from the world is not geographical separation. In John 17:14–18, Jesus talks about how the disciples are not of this world and how he has sent them into the world to be salt in this world. Even though we are a small group of people, we are to influence the whole. A well-known sociologist from America has said that if 2 per cent of the population are totally dedicated to morality, they can change that whole nation. I don't know how true that is but certainly that's very challenging; we are salt, we are leaven, a small group of people but we go into the world and we make a difference for Christ.

You are sent to a specific location by God. Wherever you are, you have been put there by God and God is calling you to be his presence in that place. All the different churches, all the different places, go to form God's beautiful mosaic that he has created in this world. In the book of Acts we have beautiful stories of how the same unchanging gospel was presented in unique and different ways because people were different. The same gospel went to them but there was a cultural beauty in the variety in which the gospel was presented to these people. So Christians have a theology of place – we believe that the place where God put us is important.

● *Does it change your perspective on where you live, knowing it is where God has called you and placed you?*

● *Do you have people of different cultural backgrounds in your group? Ask them to come up with ways in which the gospel could be effectively presented in their culture.*

What they were

Then, Christians are believers. Paul says 'To the saints who are in Ephesus and are faithful in Christ Jesus . . .' (1:1). This word probably means believers in Christ Jesus, rather than faithful people. Belief is how we enter the kingdom of God. Over and over again in the Bible we are told this – to be born again we must believe.

What's so special about belief? Is it just uttering some magic words which change our lives forever? No. What happens when we believe is that we reverse what took place in the Garden of Eden. Adam and Eve ate of the tree of the knowledge of good and evil. When they took of that tree, they were saying: 'We will decide for ourselves what is good and what is evil.' They chose to be independent of God. They said, 'We can save ourselves by our efforts.' That's the heart of sin: pride or independence from God.

In this independent way we can achieve great heights as humans and we can admire those achievements. But in some way, even those great heights can be an expression of human rebellion against God, because they are done independently of God. God says, 'Don't try to run your own life. Come to me and let me run your life for you. Let me be the Lord of your life.' When we believe, what we are doing is giving back the fruit to God. We realise we can't save ourselves: we have tried and we have failed. We are turning from our independence and telling God, 'Please save us, please help us, please be the Lord of our lives.'

We live on our own, try to run our own lives and then realise it doesn't work and when we turn, there is God to accept us.

● *In what circumstances do you find it easy to fully rely on God? And when do you find it very hard?*

Who they were in

That phrase 'In Christ Jesus' was a favourite expression of Paul's. The great Scottish theologian James S. Stewart has written a book about Paul and entitled it *A Man in Christ*.[8] That's one of the great points in Paul's theology. Statements like 'in Christ', 'in Christ Jesus', 'in the Lord', 'in him' come 164 times in Paul's writings and thirty-six times in the book of Ephesians. Sometimes it's talking about what we get because of Christ: chapter 1:7 says 'In him we have redemption . . .' But usually what Paul is saying is that we are in Christ, we are in union with Christ, we are united to him, we live in him and for him.

There was an old man who was very poor: he lived in a 'poor house' as they used to call it in those days. He was bent in two and someone went to visit him and told him, 'It must be hard for you to live in this poor house.' The man slowly lifted himself up and said, 'I don't live in this poor house; I live in God.' Our life is saturated with God, with Jesus.

Paul said in Philippians 1:21, 'For to me to live is Christ and to die is gain.' Now that we are in Christ, Christ marks our identity. God looks at us in Christ. Colossians 3:3 says, '. . . your life is hidden with Christ in God.' Bruce Narramore, in his book *Freedom from Guilt*[9] says that we are like a piece of paper that has been put inside a book. We are part of that book, now. The paper may have a lot of stains on it but when God looks, he sees the book and he sees us through the eyes of that book, not the dirt that is in our lives. We are now hidden with Christ in God.

We may have lived a terrible life before but God has forgiven us. Jeremiah 31:34 says 'I will forgive their iniquity, I will remember their sin no more.' The world doesn't forget; that's the hard thing; but God does. There was a woman who had lived a very bad life. And she came to Christ and as she was thinking about what it means to be a Christian, suddenly she burst out, 'In God's sight, I'm a virgin.' That's true, because God forgives and forgets. We shape our identity based on our relationship with Christ. The most important thing about us now is that we belong to Christ; we belong to his body along with other believers. It's very hard for me, being a sports fan, to watch some of the cricket games that Sri Lanka plays against Australia and England. I come to these countries to preach and I'm supposed to love these people. . . But it's true. This new identity is more important than my national identity: I'm part of the body of Christ.

We have been having a war in Sri Lanka between the Sinhalese people and the Tamil people. Early in my ministry I used to discourage Sinhalese people from marrying Tamil people, and vice versa, because the parents would get so upset about it, and one of our ministries as youth workers is to try and reconcile children with their parents. But then after some time I realised that when a Sinhalese marries a Tamil and they live together happily, they demonstrate the beauty of the body of Christ and that our races can live in harmony. So I began to talk about that publicly. Then my daughter announced that she wanted to marry a Tamil. I'm a Sinhalese. I was thrilled, my wife was thrilled. We knew that this boy loves Jesus and that was the most important thing for us.

● *Is there anyone you know who is 'living in the poor house', whatever that might mean for them, who may be encouraged to be reminded that they 'live in God'? Send them an encouraging letter, text or email.*

● *'For to me to live is Christ and to die is gain.' Is this true for you? Share your thoughts with the group.*

● *How does it make you feel, to know that God has fully forgiven you? How should we treat others in the light of that forgiveness?*

FURTHER STUDY

Look over the four points again. Discuss what each of these elements – saints; in Ephesus; believers; in Christ – means for you personally and as a group. Then read Colossians 3:1–4. How do these verses reinforce and enhance what you have learned?

REFLECTION AND RESPONSE

Reflect again on the importance of accepting what the word says about the authorship of this letter.

• 'A saint is one through whom light shines.' How can you hold that thought this week?

• Living in a village with very little Christian witness, Rachel wondered whether she should sell up and move. One day, she was reading a book and became aware of an annoying little 'lump' in the pages. That little 'lump' was one single grain of salt. God spoke to her: 'See how even one grain makes such a difference.' As you think on this, write down and then share any thoughts that come to mind.

• Nominate a speaker to read the following words whilst the rest of the group have their eyes shut: 'You come to me. Don't try to run your own life. Come to me and let me run your life for you. Let me be the Lord of your life.' Read more than once if required and spend some time in quiet, thinking and praying about these words. You may decide to have a time of open prayer and worship.

• Invite people to each write a line or a short paragraph about the most important thing they have learned today, in the group journal.

CHAPTER 3

Grace and peace

Aim: To think about the lavishness of God's grace and his peace available to us through Christ

> **FOCUS ON THE THEME**
> Grace. What does this word mean for you? Ask each
> member of the group to sum up what it means for them.
> Write down key words, thoughts and phrases. Do the same
> with the word 'Peace.' Do we think in terms of world peace
> or our own peace with God?

Read: Ephesians 1:1,2,17
Key verse: Ephesians 1:2

Paul's greeting says, 'Grace to you and peace from God our Father and the Lord Jesus Christ.' Grace and peace . . . this phrase comes in all thirteen of Paul's letters. It's obviously very important.

GRACE

The standard greeting in the Greek-speaking world was *chairein* which means 'greetings.' People would, when they met each other, say '*Chairein*, greetings.' Paul modified that *chairein* to a related word called *charis*, which is grace. He modified the standard greeting to give a distinctively Christian greeting. The word 'grace' appears 155 times in the New Testament – about a hundred times in the letters of

Paul and twelve times in Ephesians. In the New Testament, it's used to give the sense of what God has done for us in Christ Jesus and it came to have the idea of the undeserved, unmerited favour that God gives to us. In Ephesians 2:8 Paul says, 'by grace you have been saved through faith. And this is not your own doing; it is the gift of God, not the result of works, so that no-one may boast.' This is why the gospel is good news; *he did for us what we couldn't do for ourselves.*

One of the popular lexicons of New Testament Greek says that in Greek writing, very often this word *charis*, grace, was not clearly differentiated from the word meaning joy, *chara*. Joy and grace are very close to each other. The Australian Bible scholar, Leon Morris, says that the fundamental idea of grace is 'that which causes joy.' Christianity is a joyous religion because God has done so much for us. Joy is the hallmark of Christianity. Paul mentions joy second after love in his list of the fruit of the Spirit (Gal. 5:22). In the Old Testament there are about twenty-three words for joy. Zephaniah 3:14 and 17 have seven different words for joy. Our attitude to life is characterised by amazement over what God has done for us.

- *Grace is not just something we say at meal times: it is God's free, unmerited, unearned favour. Is that truth a deep reality for you?*
- *'Joy is the hallmark of Christianity' – but is it the hallmark of your life? Discuss what it means to know the freedom that comes from really believing Jesus loves you unreservedly. Encourage testimonies.*

I love the story of Billy Bray, an early Methodist preacher, who has become a hero to me. He became my hero because I work with the poor and he was from a poor background. He was a miner and he never really gave up his mining culture when he became a Christian. He would go visiting people and when he found out that a member of a household had become a Christian, he would take this person, put them on his shoulders and run round outside the house, praising God.

That is very similar to the reaction of the father when he saw his prodigal son coming home. In those days, rich men used to wear long cloaks. He saw his son coming and even though it was not culturally appropriate for elderly rich people to run on the streets, he lifted his cloak and ran towards that son. He hugged him and said, 'Kill the fatted calf, prepare a feast, let's rejoice.' The people were singing and dancing because the one who had been lost had come home. That's the glory of Christianity.

The elder brother couldn't understand this. He said, 'Look how much I have *slaved* for you' – that's the word in the Greek. 'I have worked so hard.' He was focusing on what he had done. When we focus on what we have done, we'll never be happy because all we do is inadequate. But when we realise what God has done, it fills our hearts with joy. That's what it means to live under grace.

● *God does not want us to work for him, he wants to do his work in and through us. How does this thought challenge you?*

Paul expressed a wish that his readers would have grace at the start of all his letters, so it must be very important that we develop the discipline of receiving God's grace every day. We need to keep receiving it because we can lose that sense of being graced. There is so much sin in the world that sin could be our focus. We could spend our time fighting the sins of others and being angry with the wrong that has been done. We fight wrong but we have nothing to give in its place. Today, being good has got a bad name. When you say somebody is a 'goody-goody', it's an insult. In the Bible, Romans 5:20 says 'where sin increased, grace abounded all the more.' Ephesians 1:8 says grace was 'lavished upon us' – the word has a sense of overflow; grace is greater than all our sin. And we must receive this grace daily. We fight wrong but we have something beautiful to offer to this world: a God who has loved us enough to come and die and give his life for us.

- *How would you respond in the following scenarios?*
  - *A Christian friend has decided to give up reading newspapers and sell his TV because the media is full of bad news. He asks what you think of his decision.*
  - *An elderly neighbour, a nominal churchgoer, is sitting next to you on the bus, talking about 'all the terrible things that are happening in the world.' There's no joy in her conversation.*
  - *Discuss or role-play in twos if you have the time.*

I celebrated thirty years in my job with young people about ten days ago. Many of the people I've worked with come from non-Christian, difficult and dysfunctional backgrounds. Many of them are treated as sub-human by society. To get out of the trap of poverty, many mothers have gone abroad to work, so they have to grow up without a mother. Often, the father will take the money that the mother sends and drinks and sometimes takes another woman for himself. Relatives often sexually abuse these children. They have had so much sorrow and pain and they wonder whom they can trust. We tell them: 'God loves you and he has paid the price of love.' There's been a lot of pain in this ministry – but one of the encouraging things is to see people who have been graced, whose lives have come to characterise the joy of the Lord.

- *How have you been encouraged by what grace means in your life?*

PEACE

Having modified the Greek greeting by making 'greeting' into 'grace', Paul then takes on the Hebrew greeting. The typical Hebrew greeting was *Shalom* and that means 'peace'. . . *salaam* in Arabic. The word 'peace' comes seven times in Ephesians. It has a rich meaning. Paul talks of the gospel in Ephesians 6:15 as the 'gospel of peace.' We are told that Christ preached peace and the context is the reconciling of Jews and Gentiles to God (Eph. 2:14–17). We have peace with God and so we have peace with each other. The alienation from God and from others is solved. But that doesn't come to the heart of the meaning of peace. The meaning of peace, especially in the greeting, is general well-being; wholeness; intactness; safety; spiritual prosperity. That's what God gives us. When God is with us, things are going to be fine.

Charles Spurgeon told a story about a little boy who had lost his ring. He was crying bitterly about this and then suddenly he stopped crying and he prayed. His sister said, 'What is the good of praying? Will praying bring back your ring?' The boy replied, 'No, but praying has made me quite willing to do without the ring if it is God's will. And is that not almost as good as having it?' That boy discovered peace.

This peace extends to our relationships with people and creation. Later Paul speaks about how God, in Jesus as our peace, breaks the barriers between Jews and Gentiles. Then the Bible looks forward to the time when God's *shalom* is going to cover the whole earth. In anticipation of that, we will do all we can to bring *shalom* here on earth. We become agents of peace, showing kindness, bringing peace between people, upholding justice and working as God's people.

● *Do you have a treasured possession/person/ambition/dream? Are you happy to do without it, if it is not God's will?*

● *'When God is with us, things are going to be fine.' Meditate
on this comforting thought. How can you remind yourself of
this when things get tough?*

. . . FROM GOD

Then he says 'from our God and Father and the Lord Jesus
Christ.' He puts God and Jesus together: the doctrine of the
deity of Christ was not concocted three or four centuries
after Christianity was born. It was there, right in the New
Testament. Peace and grace come from God because of
what Christ Jesus did. All of this is the result of God's action
in our life, through Christ.

A friend was visiting an elderly woman who was badly
crippled by arthritis and he asked her, 'Do you suffer
much?' She pointed to her hand and said, 'Yes, but there is
no nail here. He had the nails, I have the peace.' She pointed
to her head and said, 'There are no thorns here. He had the
thorns, I have the peace.' Then she pointed to her side and
said, 'There is no spear here. He had the spear, I have the
peace.' Peace was won for us on the cross; all because of
what Jesus did.

● *Is the peace of Christ in your heart a reality for you today?
Read again the words of the woman (above). In silence, think
about the words. If appropriate, ask Jesus to give you the
peace he promises. Trust him to do this. You may wish to
pray with someone else.*

So in conclusion, the first two verses of Ephesians chapter 1
show us some great truths about us as Christians: we are
saints, separated for God, giving up things that he dislikes,
living for God only and, in the process, reflecting what God

is like in this world. We are living for God in our location; we are believers, depending on Christ for everything and we are in Christ, our life is saturated with Christ. And there are two things we need all the time: grace, the blessings of Christ given at his expense which bring joy to our lives, and peace: peace with God, peace with fellow human beings and general well-being; a process that will culminate in all of creation, finally, expressing this *shalom* of God.

FURTHER STUDY

Read the story of the prodigal son in Luke 15:1–31. Afterwards, select one member of the group to be the interviewer and others to be the lost son, the father and the elder son. What can we learn from the attitudes of the key characters about the grace of God and the peace that he gives us through Christ?

REFLECTION AND RESPONSE

- In Focus on the theme, you were encouraged to write down what 'grace' and 'peace' mean to you. Have your ideas changed through what you have learned? Write down any new thoughts. Add these thoughts to the group journal.

- How can you, as individuals or as a group, challenge and encourage others this week with the good news of God's free, unearned favour? Pray for any people you know who are suffering and who need the joy and peace of the Lord. Pray also for members of the group who would like to be 'graced' this week.

- Praise God for his wonderful gift of grace and peace through his Son.

REVIEW OF EPHESIANS 1:1,2:

It is amazing how much we can learn from just two verses. We have discovered something of the background of the book of Ephesians; how theology will influence our Christian lives; the importance of authorship: the four things that Christians are; and our great need for God's grace and peace that are met through Jesus Christ. Think through who you are in Christ and the things that God has done for you.

POINTS TO PONDER
• What have you learned about God?

• What have you learned about yourself?

• What actions or attitudes do you need to change as a result?

CHAPTER 4

Every blessing

Aim: To examine the real meaning of blessing and being blessed

FOCUS ON THE THEME
There's a very popular saying today: 'Oh, bless.' It's a word we take very lightly. If someone sneezes, many people say 'Bless you' and we find ourselves writing 'God bless' in cards and emails. But what does 'blessing' really mean? Can we bless God? How has he blessed us? Briefly share how you feel God has 'blessed' you this week.

Read: Ephesians 1:3–6,11,12
Key verse: Ephesians 1:3

The second section of Ephesians 1 is what we call a eulogy, where Paul blesses God for blessing us, and it is a reflection of the blessings of election.

BLESSINGS OF ELECTION

Blessed be God

Paul starts by blessing God for blessing us. He says 'Blessed be . . . God.' Ephesians 1:3–14 is one long sentence in the Greek – 202 words. In his letters, after the salutation where he identifies himself and then talks about whom he's writing to, Paul usually puts a prayer, which is often a summary of the contents of the book. This prayer is normally a prayer of thanksgiving and petition and we have this later on (vv15–20). But in Ephesians there is a slight move away from the usual tradition and Paul gives what we might call a eulogy or a doxology. It follows the style of the Hebrew prayer called the *berakah*. This is often said in the synagogues during worship where people bless God for who he is.

There's a very interesting play on words in the Greek. The NIV translates this as 'Praise be to the God and Father of our Lord Jesus Christ' but the word used there is the word 'blessed.' Paul is saying, 'Blessed be God who has blessed us with every spiritual blessing', three words with the same root. The first one, 'blessed' is an adjective; 'who has blessed us' is a verb and 'with every spiritual blessing' is a noun. This word 'blessed' is an adjective, from the Greek word *eulogetos* from which we get 'eulogy.' It means worthy of being praised; blessed, commended. In the New Testament, that particular word is used only for God, while the verb is used for people – he has blessed us.

Leon Morris says, 'In humans, blessedness is the result of divine activity. In God, it is a natural attribute. And in people, it is a divine gift.' God is blessed. He gives us blessings and therefore, because we have been blessed by God, we glorify God. This often happens in the Bible: in Luke, for example, *eulogetos* is used in chapter 1:68 where Zechariah says 'Blessed' when he's praising God after they named his son John. In 2 Corinthians 1:3, Paul uses *eulogetos* after experiencing God's comfort and help in a very tough situation. As he remembered how God comforted him, he said, 'Blessed be the God and Father of our Lord Jesus Christ, the Father of mercies, the God of all comfort, who comforts us in all our afflictions' (2 Cor. 1:3,4).

● *Has there been a time that God has especially comforted you in your troubles? Thank and bless him for being there for you.*

In 1 Peter 1:3 Peter blesses God for the new birth and says 'Blessed be the God and Father of our Lord Jesus Christ. According to his great mercy, he has caused us to be born again to a living hope through the resurrection of Jesus from the dead.' These eulogies are outbursts of thanksgiving, of praise to God. Often they are almost like detours. In 1 Timothy, Paul talks about how he has been called, even though he was a blasphemer (1 Tim. 1:12,13) and there was this wonderful mercy that came to him (v14) and this glorious gospel that Christ Jesus came into the world to save sinners (v15). And then he says how he was shown mercy even though he was the biggest of sinners (v16). After having said that, he bursts into praise: 'To the King of ages, immortal, invisible, the only God, be honour and glory for ever and ever. Amen' (v17). Then he goes back to what he was talking about before!

When Christians reflect on God's goodness, they burst into praise. Deborah does this in Judges, after her great victory. Chapter 4, with twenty-four verses, describes the battle and its background. Then in chapter 5 there are *thirty-one* verses giving a song of praise for victory in battle. In Jonah chapter 2, Jonah thought he was dead and realises he's alive. He praises God for eight verses.

We need to learn to stop our busy activities to meditate on the glory of God and how it has expressed itself in our lives. This doxology on great theological truths is a wonderful passage, getting deeper and deeper into the heart of what God has done for us.

● *Do you ever pause in the middle of your busy schedule just to meditate on the glory of God and how his love has expressed itself within your life? Try to do so over the coming week.*

Some cultures lend themselves a little better to this type of meditative conversation than others. During the last cricket series that we had between England and Sri Lanka, we had a Sri Lankan crew of commentators and the BBC arranged for them to give commentaries, half in English and half in Sinhalese. Even though both groups of commentators were Sri Lankans, there was a clear difference in the style of the commentary. The English commentary would be very analytical and accurate in describing what was happening. The Sinhalese commentary was full of adjectives – 'this beautiful . . . lovely to behold . . . skilful . . . well-timed . . . bullet-like' – to describe just one stroke. That is partly because the Eastern culture is less efficiency-oriented. We learn efficiency from the West – we desperately need to learn that because our cultures are not very efficient. But the one advantage we have is that our type of language is more prone to meditation. We need to discipline ourselves to slow down, to think about God. When we do so, we realise how glorious he is and we burst forth into praise.

● *Often, western Christians shy away from the idea of 'meditation' because of its connections with eastern belief systems. What is Christian meditation and how can you incorporate it into your daily Quiet Time? What benefits do you think you might discover as a result?*

Blessed in Christ

In Ephesians 1:3 Paul says, 'Blessed be the God and Father of our Lord Jesus Christ.' In the Old Testament, the people often described God as the God of their fathers: of Abraham, Isaac and Jacob. We have an even greater incentive to praise. This God whom we praise is the Father of our Lord Jesus Christ. Jesus gave a human face to God. He showed us what true love is like. The Israelites trusted the God of Abraham and Isaac and Jacob and there were wonderful stories of covenant love that they could look back to. But how much more we know in the New Testament. Jesus brought salvation straight into our individual lives through his life, death, resurrection and exaltation.

Paul says that he has 'blessed us in Christ.' The phrase 'blessed us' is the verb from *eulogeo* and the expression 'in Christ' occurs twelve times in these twelve verses, describing things that come to us because of what Christ has done. The beauty of the Trinity is at work here. God has initiated this and Christ has made it possible for us to experience these blessings. Later on, we will see how the Holy Spirit comes and makes them real in our lives.

● *Think about false ideas of what God is like – ideas that are prevalent in today's society (for example, an ineffectual old man; an angry, vengeful deity). How might people begin to think differently if they understood that Christ gave God a human face? How can you show this picture of God to people you know who are not yet Christians?*

We are told that he has made available to us 'every spiritual blessing' – everything which gives us the full life that God intends for us. Yet we find this so hard to believe. We sometimes feel deprived and angry about the things we encounter and it doesn't seem as if we are having every spiritual blessing. 'Every' is a comprehensive term – everything we need is there. Why is it then that we often complain as if things have gone wrong? We complain because the world and its values have become our focus.

● *Praise God that he gives us every spiritual blessing for the full life he intends for us. But be real. Is this something you find hard to believe, especially in times of trial?*

● *Spend some time examining your own focus in life. Is it Christ? Is it the world? Or is it a mixture?*

Blessed in the heavenly realms

Paul says that 'every spiritual blessing' (3) is given to us in the heavenly places or, as the NIV puts it, in 'heavenly realms.' This term occurs five times in the book of Ephesians. This is the sphere in which the principalities and powers which we battle operate (Eph. 6:10–18). We are not talking about heaven per se; John Stott calls this 'the unseen world of spiritual reality.'

In the biblical worldview, there are different realms that are important for us to take into consideration. There is the intellectual realm, the material realm and the spiritual realm. For example, when someone is converted, there may be an intellectual battle, where we seek to convince them of the truth so that they are persuaded to accept Christ. Then there are material issues; very often when Christians show concern for someone's needs, that person becomes open because the material benefits they received orient them towards hearing the gospel. Then there are spiritual battles in people coming to Christ. Satan keeps their eyes blinded so that they will not see. In the process of evangelism, we pray and we battle Satan so that Satan's hold upon them will be taken away. So prayer is part of the work that we do in the spiritual realm. Or perhaps someone is depressed. This could be because they have a real material need – such as being unable to feed their children. You would need to give them material help. Or perhaps they have emotional wounds and we are now entering the psychological realm or even the realm of psychiatric care. But sometimes people are depressed because of demonic influence. If so, we pray and battle with Satan until freedom comes.

- '*Some Christians are always seeing demons.*' *That's true but we neglect the truth of the spiritual realm at our peril. Do you ever find yourself rationalising spiritual powers away? Ask God to give you discernment, so you will be aware of the principalities and powers that we fight. Praise Jesus that he has overcome the forces of darkness.*

- *In coming to Christ, there can be intellectual, material and spiritual barriers. How would you show the reality of Jesus to the following spiritual seekers:*

  - *University student Jamie: 'A loving God wouldn't send anyone to hell. In fact, why would a loving God make a hell in the first place?' How would you answer Jamie's intellectual queries?*

  - *Kate isn't a committed Christian but she's interested. She can't always regularly attend church as she's divorced, has two small children and her own mother, a widow, is ill and alone and often calls on her daughter for help and company. How would you show Christ to Kate?*

  - *Margaret has been a regular church attendee and choir member for the best part of forty years. But when you speak to her about being 'born again' and 'knowing Jesus', she doesn't seem able to hear you. One day, she tells you that as a teenager she was very involved in séances. How would you lead Margaret to Christ?*

There are different realms in which we live and all are important. However, Paul seems to be telling us that if we are filled in the spiritual realm, we can endure hardship in the other realms and we will be satisfied.

There was an old woman who lived in a cottage and one day she had nothing but a piece of bread and water as a meal. Lifting up her hands, she said as a blessing, 'What, all this and Christ too?' She had fullness in the spiritual realm. Charles Spurgeon, who tells this story, was one of the greatest preachers of the nineteenth century but he was prone to depression. He said: 'I, of all men, am perhaps the subject of deepest depression at times. Yet, there lives not a person who can say more truthfully than I, my soul doth magnify the Lord and my spirit has rejoiced in God my Saviour.'

Heavenly truths helped him with this particular problem – which was probably a personality problem, something that he would not be free from until he got to heaven. But he was able to face it and experience God's victory in the midst of it.

● *If you know someone who is feeling low, contact them this week to see how they are coping. Offer to pray for them and with them. Is there any practical help you can give them?*

FURTHER STUDY
Sometimes we struggle to see ourselves as blessed. We might find we are even struggling with God, as Jacob did (see Gen. 32:26). We can be comforted to know that we are already blessed in Christ and can therefore rest in his complete and finished work. Read the Beatitudes (Mt. 2:3–11; Lk. 6: 20–26) and discuss Jesus' perspective on who is truly blessed – and who is not. How do the Beatitudes encourage you in your own situation? Also, look at Luke 7:23. How does this challenge you?

REFLECTION AND RESPONSE
• We are blessed in the 'heavenly realms with every spiritual blessing in Christ.' How aware are you of the unseen spiritual dimension in your daily life – and the life of your town and nation? Are you more aware of it now than you were before? Reflect, discuss and pray for anyone who is fearful. You may also like to pray for individuals and situations known to you where 'powers' seem to be at work.

- 'Jesus brought salvation straight into our individual lives through his life, death, resurrection and exaltation. So we are told that he has blessed us in Christ.' Think of what Christ has done for you. Bless God by writing a short prayer, hymn or poem of praise. Read it out to the group if you wish.

CHAPTER 5

God's choice, our responsibility

Aim: To examine the implications of predestination and the responsibility of election

FOCUS ON THE THEME
Improvise a quick sketch about 'Gloria Introductions Agency', where someone is trying to introduce a person to Jesus. Then it's time to think about your testimonies again. Can you see how Christ was pursuing you in love through people, circumstances, events in your life, before you came to know him? Thank God for the people who were key in introducing you to Jesus.

Read: Ephesians 1:3–6,11,12
Key verses: Ephesians 1:4,5,11

GOD'S CHOICE

In verse 4, Paul talks about election and predestination: 'even as he chose us in him, before the foundation of the world, that we should be holy and blameless before him.' He chose us. That emphasises that salvation is not our action; God decided to give us salvation. In verse 5, another word comes in – predestined: 'He predestined us for adoption through Jesus Christ, according to the purpose of his will.' Verse 11 repeats it: 'In him we have obtained an inheritance, having been predestined according to the purpose of him who works all things according to the counsel of his will.' Predestination has the sense that he had a definite plan for us and he's going to fulfil this plan. Paul is saying that the sole authority and initiative for salvation is God's. *Chosen* focuses on the people elected, *predestination* focuses on God's purpose for those people.

● *How does it make you feel to know that you are chosen by God?*
● *How does it make you feel to know that God has a definite plan for your life?*

The church is going to debate the mechanics of this until Christ comes back. And it's important for us to do so. Is Paul talking about the election of individuals to salvation? Or about corporate election of the people of God? Do those who don't believe have no chance at all, ever, of salvation? What role do humans have in this process? What responsibility do they bear? Can they resist the call of God when God calls them? Proverbs 25:2 is a very comforting verse. 'It is the glory of God to conceal things but the glory of kings to search things out.' Grappling with issues like this greatly enhances our growth and understanding of God and his ways.

What are the implications of the thrust of this passage? Firstly, there is a strong emphasis on God's initiative in granting us salvation. The two words 'chose' and 'predestined' indicate this and then verse 5 says 'according to the purpose of his will.' Verse 11 adds 'according to the purpose of him who works all things according to the counsel of his will.' Those who are saved are saved because of God's decision to call them to himself, because salvation is not primarily our decision. We must believe and decide but the strength for that believing and deciding comes from God for that believing and deciding. He gives us grace to respond to his love.

● *Is there someone you are praying for to know the Lord? Pray that God will give them grace to respond to his love.*

The church will battle as to whether that grace could be resisted or whether it is irresistible but whatever side one is on, in the theological spectrum of the church, all biblical Christians believe that God gives the grace for us to believe.

John 15:16 says: 'You did not choose me but I chose you and appointed you that you should go and bear fruit.' There's a very good book on Ephesians called *The Genius of Grace* by Sam Gordon.[10] He talks about a boy who was asked, 'Have you found Jesus?' The boy scratched his head and thought for a moment and said, 'I didn't know Jesus was lost. But I can tell you what I do know. I was lost and he found me.'

GOD'S WORK

Election focuses on God's initiative and, secondly, it also gives us confidence in our witness. If this is God's work, we are to do our part as well as we know how. God uses persuasion to bring people to himself. And in order to persuade people, we study the gospel, we study the way people think so that we can communicate the gospel in ways that are understandable and convincing to them. We study their culture so that the form in which the gospel is presented is one with which they are familiar. There's a lot of work that we do in order to communicate the gospel effectively. But because it is God who brings people to himself, we leave the rest to God.

In my early years in ministry, I used to be terrified when I had to give an invitation to people to come to Christ. I would wonder, 'Will they come?' All sorts of questions would go through my mind. Then this Methodist talked to a Presbyterian evangelist, Leighton Ford, and he told me, 'This is God's work. Why are you terrified? You leave it to God. You do your part and God will do the rest.' That gave me great release in my evangelistic ministry, to know that this is God's work. I do my part and God will do the rest. We leave it to him.

● *If we understand that the conversion of others is not totally down to us, how might this affect our work and witness in evangelism?*
● *St Stephen's Church is planning an outreach. The minister asks Bob if he will help to give out literature in the shopping centre. 'No way. If they're meant to get saved, they will. They don't need me giving them tracts.' If you were the minister, how would you counsel Bob – perhaps using Jesus' Great Commission (Mt. 28:19,20)?*

Thirdly, election takes away our pride. Conversion was not some heroic decision that we made. Very often testimonies are given that glory in one's pre-Christian life, so that finally everybody is impressed by the heroic decision the speaker has made to follow Christ. Sometimes people can be critical of others who don't respond in the same way that they responded. My primary work is with drug addicts. We have to be very careful that these people don't get too proud about their amazing testimonies. They can ride on their testimony but there is a lot of hard work that they have to do in winning back their children, their wives, their families. They can go from church to church sharing their testimony when they should be working on their families. I see them becoming very critical of others and proud of the way they are following Christ, and I get very scared because the Bible says that pride goes before destruction. Salvation is God's work and there's no place for pride.

Fourthly, election also gives us a strong sense of security. We know how fickle we are. If it depended on us, our salvation would be on a very shaky foundation. But when God called us to himself, he knew that he could help us to follow him right to the end.

Paul says that the election is in Christ before the foundation of the world. Three times he says it's in Christ and then he says (v4), 'even as he chose us in him before the foundation of the world.' Before the world was created, there was a cross in the heart of God. God didn't decide to send Christ into the world after he found that humans had sinned. He knew that we would sin even before he created the world and he had already provided a way of escape. 1 Peter 1:19 –20 says, 'The Lamb without blemish, he was foreknown before the foundation of the world but made manifest in these last days.'

I think there's something there for us to note when we answer questions regarding the problem of evil – this is one of the most difficult questions that we encounter as people think about whether there is a God. We have to bring into our response to this question the fact that the fall was envisaged before creation and a solution was provided.

● *Before the world was founded, God had the cross in his heart. How does this powerful thought make you want to respond to him?*

GOD'S PURPOSES: ELECTION

Verse 4 says, 'even as he chose us in him before the foundation of the world, that we should be holy and blameless before him.' That presents the responsibility of election. Sin made us unholy and unclean. Salvation makes us holy. Sin made us guilty before God. Salvation makes us blameless. How is this possible?

When we are justified, we are acquitted of guilt and declared blameless. We are declared righteous – that is the meaning of justification, 'just as if' we had not sinned. God treats us just as if we had not sinned. Theologians battle over how this happens and what happens with righteousness. The Bible says that Christ's righteousness is imputed, is given, to us (1 Cor. 1:30). '[God] is the source of your life in Christ Jesus, whom God made our wisdom and our righteousness and sanctification and redemption' (1 Cor. 1:30). 2 Corinthians 5:21 says: 'For our sake he made him to be sin who knew no sin, so that in him we might become the righteousness of God.' We become righteousness in Christ. Christ's righteousness is imputed to us and then, gradually, our nature becomes conformed to Christ's image.

Romans 8:28–30 talks about the aims of election. Paul says God predestined us to become 'conformed to the image of his Son.' There may be a process involved as we appropriate this into our behaviour. Martin Luther says that salvation is like when a person has a terrible sickness and is going down and down. Then they find out what the sickness is and there is a specific medicine for that particular sickness. The person is given that medicine and while they do not immediately get well, after that sickness has been diagnosed and the correct medicine prescribed, little by little they do begin to go upwards towards wholeness.

That's what happens with us. 1 John 1:7–9 says if we walk in the light, then when we sin, we have to confess our sins. And God cleanses us of our unrighteousness through the blood that Christ has shed. When we confess our sin, we are cleansed. The Holy Spirit indwells us and makes it possible for us to overcome sin. Gradually, sin loses its hold on us. Later in Ephesians, Paul will speak on how we must put off the old nature and put on the new nature (Eph. 4:20–32). Paul uses two words in Ephesians 1:4: 'holy' which puts it positively; 'blameless' which puts it negatively. Blameless means without spot or blemish. Note that we are to be blameless '*before him*.' We can't compare ourselves with others. Our standards are God's standards.

● *Do you ever compare yourself with other Christians? How can you remember this week that the standard for holiness is Jesus Christ himself?*

When Paul talks about being blameless before him, he could be talking about our perfected state, when we are presented to him as the Bride is presented to the Bridegroom. When the Bible uses that metaphor, always it's used in the context of being holy and being ready (see Ephesians 5:25). So, if we are Christ's bride, to be presented as holy and blameless to him, then we must be holy ourselves. This is not just something that we forget about and then all of a sudden we are translated from being terrible sinners to being holy people. John, in his first letter, says we are going to see him and when we see him, we are going to be like him. Then in 1 John 3:3, he says, '. . . everyone who has this hope in him purifies himself [even] as he is pure.' In Hebrews 12:14, the author says, 'Strive for . . . holiness without which no-one will see the Lord.' The prospect of standing before God causes us to strive to be holy. Ephesians 4:1 talks about walking in a manner worthy of the calling to which we have been called. 2 Peter 1:10, talking about godliness, says, 'Be all the more diligent to make your calling and election sure.' Those who have been called have the responsibility to live holy lives. Of course, God gives us the strength to do that.

Mahatma Gandhi didn't like the Christian doctrine of salvation through grace. He admired Jesus but he didn't like the doctrine about the death of Christ bringing forgiveness to people. He said people get saved and then go and live any way they want. I'll never forget one of my classmates in school telling me 'You're a lucky guy. You people can go and do anything you want and then you go and ask God to forgive you.' That is not Christianity.

● *How would you answer someone who said you were lucky because you could do anything you liked, as God would forgive you for it and you could go and do it again?*
● *Do you ever feel tempted to give in to sin because 'God will forgive me anyway'?*

Holiness is the consuming passion of the true Christian and it's what we pray about all the time: 'Oh God, make us holy.' We talk about this with our friends. We ask for prayer about our holiness. We are accountable to others regarding our lives and we confess to and use those we are accountable to, to help us to grow in the faith. We need to have friends to help us in our holiness, because of the complexity of life nowadays. That's one of the themes of Ephesians: we don't become holy alone. We do it together.

● *Do you have someone you are accountable to? If not, perhaps you could pray about it and ask someone you know and trust as a mature Christian if they would be willing to be your 'accountability partner.' Alternatively, would it be possible to be accountable to the group you are in?*

I have a group that I'm accountable to. Wherever I go, I send a text message to them reporting how I'm faring. I sent them a very relieved text message when I came to

Keswick: 'There are only five television channels. Thank God, there is no cable television.' I'm accountable to them for my behaviour when I travel.

I wish there were more songs today on holiness, on the need to be godly people, that would instil within us the burden to become holy people. It was a priority for Paul. Some years ago I made a topical study of some of Paul's great themes and tried to see how many verses dealt with the different themes. I found that, of the 2,005 verses in the writings of Paul, there were 1,400 – that is over 70 per cent – that dealt with godliness or holiness. That's how important it was for Paul.

A.W. Tozer said, 'Go to God and have an understanding. Tell him that it is your desire to be holy at any cost. Then ask him never to give you more happiness than holiness.' Actually, happiness is holiness; you can't be happy if you're not holy, because we were made to be holy. So when we are not holy, we are being sub-human – and when you are sub-human, you can't be happy.

The founder of the seminary where I studied was a preacher called Henry Clay Morrison. He said this: 'God never fixed me up so that I could not sin. He fixed me up so that I couldn't sin and enjoy it.' That's the way God made us. Holiness is happiness.

FURTHER STUDY

Read 1 Corinthians 1:30,31 and 2 Corinthians 5:21. Think through the implications of Christ being our righteousness, holiness and redemption. His imputed nature leaves no room for boasting about our own religious goodness. How does this challenge you as an individual and as a group? Then read Romans 8:28–30. In pairs, discuss ways you are being conformed to the likeness of Jesus.

REFLECTION AND RESPONSE

- How proud are you of your own testimony? Do you ever glory in the fact that 'you chose' to turn to Christ? Do you glory in your past failings, even with the best of motives? Pray that in the future, you will make Christ the centre of your testimony, so all the glory goes to him.

- 'Holiness is the consuming passion of the true Christian and it's what we pray about all the time. "Oh God, make us holy." We talk about this with our friends. We ask for prayer about our holiness.' How far is this true for you?

- Write a prayer, asking God to help you live a holy life this week. Tuck it in your Bible or place in a prominent spot in your home so you can remember it.

- How might what you have learned today be of help in any existing evangelistic work you are involved in? If your church is not currently involved in outreach, pray about it and brainstorm ideas of how you might reach your community with the message of God's love.

- Write out the verse 1 Corinthians 1:30 in the group journal and add thoughts, creative prose or illustrations on the theme 'Holiness is happiness.'

CHAPTER 6

Our Father, our mission

Aim: What has he chosen us for?

FOCUS ON THE THEME
Last time, we looked at what Paul said about predestination and election. Today we are going to look at the privilege and mission of election. Think of the word 'privilege.' What does this word mean (a) to you (b) in society today? In what ways are we 'privileged' as Christians? Discuss. What do you believe is our 'mission' as disciples of Christ?

Read: Ephesians 1:3–6,11,12
Key verses: Ephesians 1:4–6,12

GOD'S PURPOSES

The privilege of election

Holiness gives us the responsibility of election; adoption gives us the *privilege of election*. Verse 5: 'He predestined us for adoption through Jesus Christ, according to the purpose of his will.' We were predestined for adoption.

The practice of adoption was not very common in Israel at that time but it was common in the Graeco-Roman world. It was common to adopt adults rather than children and the key to adoption was the transfer of one's income. Adoption was concerned with inheritance: if someone had no children and wanted to leave their inheritance to somebody, they would adopt and give that person the full privileges of being their child.

God had his own Son, Jesus Christ but he still chose to adopt us as his children and to give us his inheritance. This is one of the most glorious things about the gospel. In his great book, *Knowing God*, probably one of the greatest books that were written in the last century, J.I. Packer asked the question: 'What is a Christian?'[11]

● *'What is a Christian?' Go around the group, one by one, so everybody gets a chance to give a brief answer.*

He answered 'The question can be answered in many ways but the richest answer I know is that a Christian is one who has God for his Father. You sum up the whole New Testament religion if you describe it as the knowledge of God as one's holy Father.'

It will take a lifetime for us to understand the full implications of what it means to be a son or a daughter of God. Sin has had all sorts of affects on our lives and has caused us to become imbalanced, unhealthy people and it may take a whole lifetime for those things to be taken away. But the key of overcoming this lies in understanding that we are children of God.

We may have experienced so much rejection in the world that it is hard for us to accept that God loves and accepts us like this. Deep down, we don't think that we are lovable. We think we are not worthy of receiving this inheritance. But he does love us; he wants to give us his inheritance; not because we deserve it but simply because he loves us.

One of the most beautiful words in the Bible is 'delight.' We are often asked to delight in God, to delight in the Scriptures and things like that. I have found eight times in the English Standard Version of the Bible where we are told that God delights in us. He delights in us. He looks at us and says, 'That's my boy' or 'That's my girl'. Have you ever gone to see your son or daughter perform or do something in public? Your daughter comes to the platform and your heart is beating faster than hers. She's supposed to be singing but she's looking to see whether you're there. And then she sings – and the parent's heart is filled with joy. Delight: God delights in us.

● *How easy do you find it to accept that God loves you and wants to give you his inheritance? If you struggle with this idea, spend some time thinking about the meaning of 'grace' – God's free, unmerited favour. He accepts us because he loves us, not because we deserve it. How might studying the character of God help you further in accepting his unmerited love?*
● *Think of ways you can share God's delight in each one of you this week.*

It may take time for us to accept such love, if we have faced rejection. We can't believe that we are lovable and if we don't know this, we'll end up jealous, bitter and angry with the world; judgemental, always finding fault with others, unhappy, always getting hurt. If we haven't experienced the greatness of God's love, we may interpret many of the actions of others as personal rejection. But when we have experienced that love, we can face this because God's love is greater than all the rejection and hurt that people inflict on us.

● *Have you experienced the greatness of God's love for you? If not, ask someone to pray with you, that you might know that love in reality this week.*

One of the great mistakes that my denomination made was to fail G. Campbell Morgan when he went for his trial sermon, when he was preparing to be a preacher. They had a trial sermon for prospective preachers and Campbell

Morgan, the great Bible teacher, preached and they failed him. He was really down and felt that everything was bleak for him. He sent a telegram to his father giving the news, and it had one word: 'Rejected.' Quickly the father responded with another telegram: 'Rejected on earth. Accepted in heaven.' Campbell Morgan didn't give up; he became a Congregationalist. And he became a great preacher – some people think, the greatest Bible teacher of his era.

● *Rejected: have you ever felt the bleakness of rejection? Be encouraged by the story of Campbell Morgan and remember, you are accepted in heaven. Has anyone in the group got a story of rejection turned into triumph? Share it now.*

Sometimes we find ourselves praying for people: 'Oh God, how can we convince these people that you love them? That you delight in them?' How important it is for us to get people to understand the glory of adoption. So many people have come from dysfunctional homes; they've grown up without a father figure or with a terrible father and they don't want to think of God as Father. Therefore some people say, 'Don't talk about God as Father because they'll never understand it.' But I would say, 'True, they will not understand it, but we must teach them.' Because, deep down in every human heart, there is a yearning for a father, for someone who truly cares. They need to understand it and when they do, it is good news to them.

● *'My father abandoned me before I was born. When my mum told him she was pregnant, he didn't want to know. I can relate to Jesus as my friend but not God as Father.'*
● *'When I was a kid, my dad was away a lot but even when he was at home, he always seemed too busy to bother with me. I do believe in God but I can't believe he cares about the intimate details of my life.'*

- *'My dad was always angry and blaming me. Nothing I did was ever good enough for him, however hard I tried. If God's like a father, I don't want to know.'*
- *How would you talk to the above, if you wanted to share God as Father with them?*

I think of a young man who is very close to me right now. He comes from a very unusual background – his family sold illicit liquor in their neighbourhood and some of his brothers were and are drug addicts. His father died and then his mother got sick, and he was wondering, 'Who's going to look after me if my mother dies?' He was a Buddhist but he started going to Hindu temples and shrines, asking the various gods to look after him.

Around this time, our Youth for Christ volunteers would come to his neighbourhood and invite the young people for a programme. When he saw them coming, he would rush out of the back door, because he didn't want to come to the programme. Finally, they got him to come and he argued and argued about the gospel. He went on a camp and argued at that camp. He came back without accepting Christ. Later he went on another camp and argued at that camp too. Here one of the preachers quoted a verse from Scripture, Isaiah 49:15: 'Can a woman forget her nursing child, that she should have no compassion on the son of her womb? Even these may forget, yet I will not forget you.' Suddenly, he realised 'This is the God I'm looking for', and he became a Christian.

The process of healing took him a long time because he had so many wounds from his background but gradually God began to make him a whole person. Today he's a full-time worker, reaching people like him, troubled young people, with the gospel of Christ. Often when he prays, he uses the Sinhala word that is the equivalent in English of 'Daddy.' I couldn't use that word when I talk to God but for some reason when he prays, that's the word he wants to use, because God has become his Father and filled up the emptiness that he had.

● *Do you know any young person who needs to know God as their Father? Pray for them.*

God often uses different means to give us this sense of adoption. The Bible calls it the witness of the Spirit, whereby 'the Spirit himself bears witness with our spirit that we are children of God' (Rom. 8:14–17). He does it through the Scriptures; he does it through the acceptance of the Christian community. For me, it came through the fact that God had given me gifts. I was a very nervous person who never liked to talk in public, I wouldn't open my mouth. When I thought I was going to be a preacher, I dared not tell anyone because I thought they'd laugh. 'How can this fellow, who doesn't know how to open his mouth, ever preach?' But God gave me the desire to preach so I started writing sermons secretly. I live near the sea so, at night, I would go to the beach and, when there was no-one around, sit on the rocks and preach. Through this gift that God gave me, I began to realise that I am significant, I am important to him. I felt like a child.

Sometimes this sense of adoption takes place through counselling and the healing of our wounds. Sometimes it comes through a marvellous provision of God. We will never fully accept all the implications of adoption until we get to heaven. But one of the most important aspects of growth for Christians is growth in the understanding of what it means to be loved by God, what it means to be a child of God.

● *Do you agree that one of the most important aspects of growth is in understanding what it means to be loved by God? Do you feel significant, important to him?*

- *In what ways has God revealed the sense of adoption in your own life?*

THE MISSION OF ELECTION

The third thing about election is given to us in verses 6 and 12. Verse 6 says, 'to the praise of his glorious grace, with which he has blessed us in the Beloved.' Verse 12 says, 'so that we who were the first to hope in Christ might be to the praise of his glorious grace' – we live to the praise of God's grace. This is *the mission of election.*

There was a responsibility, holiness; there was a privilege, adoption; and now there's a mission: we live for God's glory. The wording here is beautiful. It says in verse 6 that when people look at us, they are going to praise God's grace. Verse 12 says that when people look at us, they are going to praise God. They praise God's glory; they are going to give glory to God. Some people look at us and say, 'What a glorious thing grace is.' Other people look at us and say, 'What a glorious God this God is.'

One of my favourite pastimes is watching cricket on television. Often what thrills me more than anything else is the artistry of cricket. Some people say 'What a boring game, going on for days and days.' But there's artistry; you see this beautiful stroke, exquisitely timed; what a great catch, what a masterly ball. What you are saying is, 'What a great game this is. What beautiful artistry there is here.' It's the same with God's grace in us. People look at us and say, 'What a wonderful thing grace is.' Then they look at us and say 'What a wonderful Person God is.'

- *What a wonderful thing grace is; what a wonderful Person God is. Spend a few moments reflecting on these statements.*

The wording in verse 6 is very unusual. Literally it's says, 'For the glory of the grace with which he has graced us.' One commentary puts it like this: 'We have been be-graced with grace.' F.F. Bruce puts it like this: 'The grace which he has lavished upon us.' There is the sense of a lavish supply of grace. That's a theme that comes all the time in the Bible. Sin is great and serious but grace is greater: God's grace super-abounds. In 1 Timothy 1:14 Paul says that even though he was a blasphemer, 'the grace of our Lord overflowed for me.' I studied this at a time when I was broken by sin that had appeared in our work. After studying this, I had to rush to a disciplinary inquiry. It was a very sad time for me. But even as I was having this sorrow, here I was, reading about the greatness of grace – greater than all the sin that people have committed. So before I went, I decided to sing the song *Wonderful grace of Jesus, greater than all my sin*.

In 2004, the church in Sri Lanka faced a lot of hostility because people were coming to Christ. There was an attempt to bring in legislation to prevent what was called 'unethical conversion.' Over one hundred churches had been hit in some way; some burnt, some with furniture destroyed, and some Christians were assaulted. It was a very bad year for us as a church. Then the tsunami hit and the Christians began to work. All sorts of terrible stories had been told about Christians, then people saw the Christians working, staying up at night, doing menial work, things that others don't like to do, working and working and working.

There was one temple that had caused a lot of trouble to a church nearby that year and that temple was hit by the tsunami. The thing that people disliked most doing was cleaning up the debris; it seemed to be an unending task. The pastor of the church that had been hit by that temple said, 'Let's clean up the temple' and the pastor joined his members as they went to clean the temple. The chief priest of that temple said, 'I did this and this and this to you and you have come and done this to me. I am very sorry for what I did.'

● *How can you do good this week to someone who has hurt you?*

'We were the first to hope in Christ' (v12). We point people who haven't yet hoped in Christ to the glory of God and his gospel.

There was a great missionary to the South Pacific Islands called John Selwyn. He had a home where he had children – and there was one child there who was particularly disobedient. He had to be disciplined quite often. One day when he was scolded by John Selwyn, he slapped John Selwyn in the face. Selwyn decided he was not going to do anything about it. He just turned and left. And this boy went from bad to worse until finally he had to be sent home.

Many, many years later, there was an old man – this boy – who was sick and who asked for a minister to come because he wanted to become a Christian. So the minister trained and taught him and then he was ready for baptism. He asked him, 'Do you want to take a new name now that you have become a Christian?' That man said, 'Call me John Selwyn because I found out what Christ was like the day that I slapped him.'

May people look at us and say, 'What a great grace, what a great God.'

FURTHER STUDY
Look at Romans 8:14–17 and Galatians 3:26–4:7. Rejoice in the fact that, whatever your background, whatever your experience with your own natural father, you are a son or daughter of God, an heir to a wonderful inheritance, with a Father in heaven who loves you.

REFLECTION AND RESPONSE

- Sin has had a damaging effect in all of our lives. People sin against us; we sin against ourselves and others; where and how we live also affects us and others. How can the understanding that we are children of God help us to live healthy, whole, balanced lives?

- Reflect on what you have learned about the responsibility, privilege and mission of election. What are some of the key issues that stand out for you in relation to yourself, your church, your wider community?

- It is possible that this study session has brought up painful issues regarding fathers/fatherhood for some people (be aware that some might also have issues with adoption). If appropriate, spend time in gentle discussion and prayer, perhaps in twos or threes. Give thanks to God for good fathers. Remember that God is the perfect Father who will never leave us or forsake us and who loves us unconditionally.

- Pray this prayer as a group: 'Lord, we know that there's a lot of disdain for your gospel in our society. We know that many people don't want to listen to what we say. But we also know that they can't help observing the way we live. O God, let our light so shine amongst our people that they may observe our good works and glorify our Father who is in heaven. Help us, O God, to be only the first-fruits of a great harvest that you're going to yield among our people. In Jesus' name we pray. Amen.'

- Finish with a hymn or song about the wonderful grace of Jesus.

REVIEW OF EPHESIANS 1:3–6,11,12:

We have learned how we bless God, as we are blessed in Christ and in the heavenly realms; we have thought about predestination and election, God's choice, his work and his purposes – the responsibility, privilege and mission of election. How is the theology of what you are learning in this series helping you in your personal Christian life, the life of the group and in the wider world? Note in the group journal.

POINTS TO PONDER

• What have you learned about God?

• What have you learned about yourself?

• What actions or attitudes do you need to change as a result?

CHAPTER 7

Paying the price

Aim: To clarify thoughts about the meaning of redemption and atonement

FOCUS ON THE THEME
Thinking back to your testimony, how much of your conversion was influenced by (a) needing Jesus in a time of crisis (b) believing what you heard about him (c) being convicted of your own sin and need of a Saviour? Discuss.

Read: Ephesians 1:7–10,13,14
Key verse: Ephesians 1:7

We have been looking at the blessings of election; we are working on some of the implications of what it means to have salvation from Christ and how that took place. Now we are going to talk about the blessings of salvation. And we start at verse 7 of Ephesians 1: 'In him we have redemption through his blood, the forgiveness of our trespasses, according to the riches of his grace . . .'

REDEEMED

This metaphor, redemption, comes from the market-place in the Graeco-Roman world, where slaves could be redeemed, freed through the payment of a price. That seems to be the primary meaning in the use of this metaphor, although even in the Old Testament there was the idea of redemption through a ransom. For example, when an ox, which was known to be dangerous, killed a person, the owner of the ox was liable to be killed, but he could redeem his life by paying a ransom. In the same way, the first-born, whether human or animal, was considered sacred to God but could be bought back by the payment of an appropriate price.

So when the Bible uses this word 'redemption' it's using the idea of buying back something. It is from that that we get the word 'ransom' in the Greek; the two words come from the same root. A ransom is a price that has to be paid in order to buy something or free somebody. Paul is using that metaphor to say that we have redemption from sin through the blood of Christ.

● *Get someone to read the following to the group: 'Zero Jones is the intrepid hero of an action thriller. The bad guy has kidnapped him and he is tied to a chair in a windowless room. 'Ha' says Zero. 'No chance of escape . . . well, looks like it's all over for me.' Yes, the situation seems hopeless. Then Zero hears footsteps. Someone's coming. A man walks into the room and cuts Zero's bonds. He leads our hero to freedom. Zero sees the man is Jesus. What do you think Zero would say to him? If you were Zero, what would you say to Jesus?*

This word 'blood' essentially refers to life. Three times in the Old Testament we are told that 'the life is in the blood' (Lev. 17:11,14; Deut. 12:23) and therefore the shedding of blood is the taking of life. So in the New Testament, it's the commonest way in which the death of Christ is mentioned. The word 'blood' is used three times as often as the word 'cross' to refer to Christ's death and five times as often as the 'death' of Christ. So obviously it's very important, because it focuses on the way the life of Christ was sacrificed.

Two great stalwarts of the evangelical movement, Alan Stibbs and Leon Morris, showed that *blood* was used for life given or taken in death and usually life violently taken.[12] That's what the Bible usually means when it uses the word blood to refer to the death of Christ. Paul is saying that this blood was like a payment for our sin.

I'm sure you've heard the familiar story but it's worth repeating because it beautifully illustrates the meaning of redemption. A little boy made a toy boat and after he had made it, he went to the lake and he let it float. Suddenly a gust of wind came and took the boat away. The poor boy sat and looked at his boat going so far that he couldn't get it back. Some days later he saw his boat in a shop and he went to the shopkeeper and said, 'This is my boat.' But the shop owner said, 'No, I bought it for money. If you want it, you'll have to buy it.' So this boy did some work, earning the money he needed, and he bought that boat. When he got it back, he told the boat, 'Now you are twice mine; I made you and now I have bought you.' That's what Jesus did with us. He made us and we went astray, and then he bought us back.

- *When you are sharing the gospel with a non-Christian relative, friend or colleague, do you emphasise the positive 'Jesus loves you. He has a great plan for your life' but find yourself glossing over the fact that Christ's blood was shed on the cross for that person? How can you share the truth of the gospel in love without appearing self-righteous or condemning?*

- *The story of the little boy and the boat is a useful story, because it not only shows us Jesus' love in redeeming us but also that human beings are not creatures independent of our Creator God. How might you use the story in sharing your faith?*

To whom was this price, the ransom for our redemption, paid? In church history there have been bizarre theories about transactions that took place between God and Satan, using Jesus as the price. Leon Morris has some wise words for us regarding this

> In the New Testament there is never a hint of a recipient. We must understand redemption as a useful metaphor which enables us to see some aspects of the great saving work with clarity but which is not an exact description of the process of salvation. We must not press beyond what the New Testament tells us about it.[13]

Such advice is helpful when we think about the death of Christ. There are a lot of figures that are used, metaphors and illustrations: none of them is complete in giving the full picture but they all add up together to give us a good idea of what happened when Jesus died.

RECONCILED

So Christ was our substitute, our atoning sacrifice. Atoning comes from the word 'atonement': that really is 'at-one-ment' and means that reconciliation was made between God and humans through what Jesus did. He was the atoning sacrifice.

The idea of Christ being a substitute, of a price paid for sin, of Jesus bearing the punishment of sin, has come under a lot of fire all through history and now recently too. Some are saying that this is not the key to understanding the death of Christ. I want to say that the work of the cross is so vast and so comprehensive that no approach does full justice to what happened. So, different people have focused on different aspects of the cross; some have focused on

Christ as Victor, where the death of Christ is looked at as a
cosmic drama through which Jesus defeated the forces of
evil (Col. 2:14,15). Gustaf Aulen wrote a book on this called
Christus Victor and says this is the classic view because this
is a view that was held for many centuries, earlier on in the
church.[14] It presents one idea – and an important idea – of
what was achieved at the cross.

   Others have focused on the appeal of the cross. This is a
subjective interpretation. And there's a lot of Scripture to
back the fact that the death of Christ is a great example and
inspiration to us, which motivates us to repentance and to
living selfless lives. But the dominant theme regarding the
death of Christ is that he was the substitute for our sins.
Paul's train of thought, here and elsewhere, and the Old
Testament context of the sacrificial system, suggest that
substitution is primary. Some explanations of this
substitutionary view have been, to some extent, inadequate.
People have used illustrations that fall short and some of
these illustrations have been irresponsible. So people have
been turned away from this view.

● *Jesus tells us to take up our cross and follow him. But his
   death meant much more than setting an example for us to
   live selfless, sacrificial lives. Why is it so important to see
   Christ as the substitute who died in our place, bearing our
   punishment?*

● *How would you answer someone who said they did not
   believe Jesus was our substitute, as they cannot believe a
   loving God would use his own Son as a substitute in this
   manner?*

Today there's less emphasis on retribution when thinking
about justice and I think that is one reason why people find
it difficult to understand the meaning of a substitutionary
atonement. People don't think of sin as something that

needs to be punished but the Bible says that sin must be punished because it's wrong. Today, when you think of justice systems, the emphasis is on the restoration of the wrongdoer and the protection of other people. Both of these are very important. So, for example, when pathological sex offenders are found, they are kept confined. At the moment there's a lot of embarrassment among the authorities in this country because somebody has been let off and he seems to have continued with his wrong actions. Restoration of the wrongdoer is also important. Restorative justice is a new field that is getting a lot of prominence recently, and I think that's very good. But the Bible also says that sin must be punished because God is just and justice requires punishment.

Sometimes we are very uneasy with statements like 'Vengeance is mine; I will repay' – the idea of the vengeance of God. I found at least seven times where the Bible speaks of vengeance in connection with God. And I found the idea of God repaying at least thirteen times. In Romans 12:19, you find both these ideas. 1 John 1:9, for example, says, 'God is faithful and just to forgive us our sins.' He is faithful because he will keep his promise to forgive. He is just because he has paid the price so that justice is served. Therefore justice is preserved when he forgives our sins. He does not lay aside his justice when he offers us forgiveness in love.

- *God sent his Son to make a substitutionary atonement for our sins; the wrath of the Father against our sin is thereby propitiated. This speaks of the enormity of God's love for us but it also speaks very eloquently of the enormity of our sin. How does meditating on God's faithfulness (1 Jn. 1:9) comfort and sustain you?*

- *Sometimes we talk about God in a 'cosy' way – 'The Big Man Upstairs' – and tend to forget that he is the awesome*

Almighty who cannot look on sin. Should we talk about God like that?

● *How different do you think TV dramas and stage plays would be if their writers or directors had had a revelation of who God really is?*

● *As you think about who God is, do you feel an extra urgency to tell people about Jesus – before it's too late?*

In my early years in ministry I used to say that when Jesus died on the cross, love overcame justice; justice said that we must be punished; love overcame this by being a greater force. When I preached that once at a missions conference in America, called the Urbana Missions Conference, a lady wrote back to me and she said, 'Don't you think this idea of love overcoming justice is not very biblical?' I realised that she was right. It is not that love overcame justice – love *satisfied* justice; love fulfilled the demands of justice. So justice was not left aside, it was satisfied when Christ died.

Joseph Bayly was one of my favourite authors. He talks about how we find it difficult to distinguish between chastisement and punishment. In the Bible, chastisement is related to the love of Christ: chastisement takes place with a view to reforming the person. Punishment is related to the wrath of God, where we see that sin has to be paid for. Both are necessary aspects of biblical truth.

● *Think of some examples of chastisement and punishment.*

Paul says that people believe in their hearts that sin must be punished. For example, in Romans 1:32 he says that disobedient people 'know God's decree that those who practice such things deserve to die.' Deep down we have this sense that sin deserves to be punished. Leon Morris talks about how even the most hardened criminal will say

'That deserves to be punished' when he sees something terrible, such as child abuse. There is that sense in all of us. Our task as evangelists is to make this sense resurface and to proclaim it in a persuasive and understandable manner, knowing that the cross and its work agree with our deepest instincts. I have felt that very strongly as we try to proclaim the gospel to Buddhists, that the cross agrees with our deepest instincts.

FURTHER STUDY
Read through one of the gospel accounts of the crucifixion (Mt. 27:32–50; Mk. 15:21–39; Lk. 23:26–47; Jn. 19:17–37). You might also like to read Isaiah 53, either with the group or alone. Thank Jesus for what he has done for you.

REFLECTION AND RESPONSE
- Spend some time in silent reflection of what Christ accomplished for you on the cross. Play a worship CD quietly in the background, if you feel this is appropriate. If anyone feels spurred to add thoughts to the group journal – perhaps just a sentence or even a word – do so as the music plays.

- If anyone is frightened by any issues raised, remind them of God's grace, the fact that he loves us so much he has made a way for us to be right with him and that he has adopted us as his children. Read together John 3:16–18 and praise God. You may wish to personalise John 3:16 and read it out loud: 'For God so loved (me) that he gave his one and only Son, that (I) who believe in him shall not perish but have eternal life.'

- 'Love satisfied justice.' Write this down on a post-it note or label and stick it to the front of your computer or on a mirror at home. Praise God whenever you see it this week.

CHAPTER 8

Seeing our need

Aim: To think about the mystery of God's plan of salvation

FOCUS ON THE THEME
Get a couple of good actors within the group to spoof a TV commercial advertising face cream. The slogan for the cream is 'Worth-it – Because I'm a good person.'

Read: Ephesians 1:7–10,13,14
Key verses: Ephesians 1:7–10

In verse 7, Paul says that we have 'redemption through his blood, the forgiveness of our trespasses' or as the NIV puts it, 'sins.' This is not the more common word for sin which comes about 173 times in the New Testament, and has the idea of falling short of the mark (*hamartia*). This is another word (*paraptoma*) that comes less often, nineteen times. This is why the RSV, NRSV, ESV and that group of translations keep the translation as trespasses. This word has the idea of taking a false step so as to lose one's footing.

What Paul is saying is that God forgives our sins. This brings another challenge to us, because people don't think that they're in need, that they are sinners who need forgiveness.

A GREAT NEED

Many constitutions have this idea of a presidential pardon or a royal pardon. Some people, when they're offered a royal pardon or a presidential pardon, refuse it because they say, 'That would mean admitting that I was guilty.' They would rather stay in prison than admit that they are guilty. I think that's the situation in the world today. Surveys done in the western world say that most of those who believe that there is a heaven and a hell expect to get to heaven, even though some of their lives are very questionable.

● *When Fran died, she had a humanist funeral. Later her boss, Mel, was telling a friend about it. 'No hymns or sermons or prayers,' she said. 'No vicars or any of that God stuff. Fran wasn't religious.' Her friend, a Christian, replied, 'Fran did come to church once when she found out she was ill. She asked Jesus to save her. So we hope to see her in heaven.' Mel was cross. 'Of course she's gone to heaven. We all go to heaven.' She didn't seem to see any contradiction in her words. This is based on a true story. How would you have answered Mel?*

● *Do you know anyone who doesn't seem to think they need forgiveness? Pray for them.*

In Sri Lanka, when you tell many Buddhists that we are all sinners, they will say 'We haven't done wrong. We are not sinners. Oh, we may have done a few wrong things but that we can overcome by working, through getting good karma. We can help ourselves. If we can't do that in this life, we'll do it in the next and the next and the next.' Even though this is a rather dreary scheme of being born many times, it has great appeal because you don't have to admit that you're helpless and ask for help. Stephen Neill says that the last thing people want is to say that they need help, that they can't help themselves.

I believe this is the reason why New Age, Buddhism, Hinduism and those kinds of religious systems are getting more and more popular in the west. The days of secular humanism are over. People want religion of some sort. But they don't want a religion that says, 'You're a sinner, you need to repent and yield to the Lordship of Christ.' These other systems tell them, 'You can do it on your own. You can grow and if you don't do it in this life, there's another life and another to help you.' So people have obliterated this truth from their life even though their consciences tell them that their sins need to be punished. And therefore we are in need of forgiveness.

- Leaf through a woman's magazine or daily newspaper. How much evidence do you find of New Age or occult beliefs?
- 'Karma: For the Hindu, the law of cause and effect which determines destiny or fate. . . . [It] teaches that for every moral or spiritual thought, word, or deed, karma produces an inevitable effect. Presumably this could not be carried out in one life; thus karma necessitates reincarnation . . . There is no forgiveness in karma. Each person must suffer for his own deeds.'[15] However many lives we live, we can never make ourselves clean. Can you think of anyone caught up in New Age beliefs? Pray for them.

Francis Schaeffer said that people have built a roof over their heads to protect them from the rays of truth that come and hit them: examples of truths that are blocked off are 'You are a sinner' or 'You are guilty.' Schaeffer says that part of our job as evangelists is to take the roof off so that people will see these truths. Christians are accused of causing psychological problems and guilt by calling people 'sinners.' This is not surprising in a world where, to many, feeling good is more important than doing right. Obviously people are annoyed when Christians talk about people being guilty before God. We have a great challenge today to engage our culture through preaching, films, novels, drama or whatever means we can find to show that there is such a thing as sin that elicits retribution. Our call is not to send people on a guilt trip, but to show them their problem so that they can experience God's freedom.

- *Many people who will not enter a church will visit a cinema, read a novel or watch a play. But Christians who are involved in creative evangelism can often feel discouraged as it is a difficult calling. As a group:*
  - *Pray that God would encourage all Christians who are involved in the media*
  - *Pray for those who are directly involved in creative evangelism – writing and acting*
  - *Pray that God will open more doors for Christian writers and dramatists*
  - *Pray for Christian novels and plays to reach a wider and more secular audience.*
  - *How can you encourage anyone in your church who is involved in drama/creative evangelism or storytelling/puppet theatre this week?*

Deep down however, people know they need forgiveness. One of America's most famous psychiatrists of the earlier generation – a man called Karl Menninger who, along with his brother, had several psychiatric hospitals – once said that if he could convince the patients in his psychiatric hospitals that their sins were forgiven, 75 per cent of them would walk out the next day.

In Sri Lanka, we had a prime minister who came from a very aristocratic and western-type background. He studied at Oxford; he was a president of the Oxford Union and then he came back to Sri Lanka to be a politician. Along with this he gave up Christianity, his family religion and became a Buddhist. When he became our Prime Minister, he gave Buddhism a very high place in the country. Buddhist monks gained new prominence. But he was finally assassinated by a Buddhist monk, and this Buddhist monk was put into prison and condemned to die. Before his execution, the monk became a Christian. He was asked, 'Why did you become a Christian?' He said the reason why he became a Christian is that there is no forgiveness in Buddhism.

● *Why do you think it is such a strong draw for people to embrace belief systems where no repentance of sins is necessary?*

My grandmother was a Buddhist and she grew up with a lot of misfortune. Her mother died when she was about four or five years old, her father died when she was in her early teens and then in her late teens she got married. She was married for ten years, had ten happy years of marriage, three children and then her husband died. People told her she was suffering for things she had done in the past, in her previous lives, and that's what her religion told her. And she was trying to offset the effects of her karma – which is the actions that produce these reactions – and she did whatever she could do to offset the karma. But it didn't work.

When she was a child, she had gone to an elementary school that was run by Christians, so she knew something about Christianity. One day, in her desperate state, she heard something like a voice telling her: 'Why don't you consider the religion that you knew as a child?' So she explored Christianity and found that she didn't have to suffer for her karma because Jesus had already suffered for her and she became a Christian.

My mother was upset for some time that her mother had become a Christian. Then she too realised that she needed forgiveness and she became a Christian. It was my mother who, many, many years later, led me to Jesus Christ. This is good news to people, even though at first they may feel they don't need it.

● *Are there any people, young or older, known to you who may have attended Sunday school/youth group but have not followed 'the religion they knew as a child'? Pray for them now.*

Verses 7 and 8 say it's 'according to the riches of his grace, which he lavished upon us, in all wisdom and insight.' This is an amazingly insightful plan, says Paul; the creation of the All-knowing, All-wise God. The atonement is God's wisdom. However, today to many people it looks like folly. Paul knew this and so he often talks about how the cross of Christ is folly to the Gentiles. In 1 Corinthians 1:18 he says, '. . . the word of the cross is folly to those who are perishing'; then in verses 23 and 24 of that same chapter he says, '. . . we preach Christ crucified, a stumbling block to [the] Jews . . . folly to [the] Gentiles but to those who are called . . . Christ the power of God and the wisdom of God.' Then in verse 25 he says '. . . the foolishness of God is wiser than men.'

Today too you see this; people think it is folly to believe this. A great New Testament theologian from Germany who had a big influence upon New Testament studies, Rudolf Bultmann, said: 'How can the guilt of one man be expiated by the death of another who is sinless . . . ? What primitive mythology it is, that a divine Being should become incarnate and atone for the sins of men through his own blood?'[16] We can expect this type of challenge to the wisdom of the cross because it has happened all through history.

Let us ask God to show us ways to show the world that this is indeed a wise message.

There was a man called Dr Charles Berry, an eminent preacher of a previous generation. He had been trained in a theologically liberal environment and he struggled with the concept of a substitutionary atonement and Christ sacrificing himself for our sins. He looked at Christ more as a moral teacher and he viewed Christianity essentially as living a good life.

In his first pastorate in England, late one night, while he was sitting in his study, he heard a knock. He opened the door and found a poorly dressed Lancashire girl. This girl said, 'Sir, are you a minister?' and he said, 'Yes.' Then she said, 'You must come quickly. I want you to get my mother in.'

He thought it was a case of a drunken woman who was out on the streets and said, 'Why don't you go and get a policeman?' She replied, 'No, my mother is dying and you must come quickly and get her in to heaven.'

The young minister went to the mother, knelt by her side and began to describe the kindness of Jesus, explaining that he had come to show us how to live unselfishly. This desperate woman said, 'Mister, that's no use for the likes of me. I am a sinner, I have lived my life. Can't you tell me of Someone who can have mercy on me and save my poor soul?'

Dr Berry says, 'I stood there in the presence of a dying woman and I had nothing to tell her. In order to bring something to that dying woman I leapt back to my mother's knee, to my cradle faith and I told her of the cross and the Christ who was able to save. Tears began running down the cheek of this woman. She said, "Now you're getting at it. Now you're helping me."' This is how Dr Berry concluded the story. He says, 'I want you to know that I got her in. And blessed be God, I got in myself.' The foolishness of man is God's wisdom.

- *It has been said: 'There are no atheists in a foxhole.' Do you think this is true? Discuss.*
- *How do you feel when someone ridicules your faith and calls it nonsense? Has this been your experience recently? Pray for the person who has ridiculed you.*

A GREAT MYSTERY

In verse 9, Paul talks about God making known to us 'the mystery of his will, according to his purpose, which he set forth in Christ.' This word 'mystery' comes five times in Ephesians. In the New Testament, it means a truth once hidden but now made known to us humans.

Apocalyptic literature is the literature that looks very much like the book of Revelation. In the first century, in apocalyptic literature (for example what was found in the Dead Sea scrolls in the Qumran caves), the idea of mystery was a secret plan of God that would become apparent at the end of the age, glimpses of which were given to special people who had special abilities. Unlocking the mystery was something that God would give to special people later on. But now, says Paul, this mystery has been unlocked by Christ. There is no need to wait till the last day in order to know what God's strategy is.

There was a heresy later on in the church called Gnosticism and it was in its early stages during the latter part of Paul's ministry, when this letter was written. Incidentally, Gnosticism is gaining acceptance today and some people are thinking that the Gnostic gospels are better representations of Christ's work than our canonical Gospels. In Gnosticism, deeper truths were revealed to special people. Paul is saying that the mystery is now open; God has disclosed it to everyone. Colossians 1:26 says: 'the mystery hidden for ages and generations but now revealed to his saints' so when we go with the gospel we must remember this: it's God's answer to the world. People have longed for this to take place and now it has happened. When we go with the gospel, we may be attacked, we may be despised, we may be called fools. We may be accused of unworthy motives. But we are giving God's message to the world.

● *Why do you think some find the idea of special knowledge or knowledge given to special people appealing?*

Jesus often said: 'The time is fulfilled.' What the prophets said will happen has now happened. I found that word 'fulfilled' used in this way twenty times in the gospels. 1 Peter 1:10–12 describes this beautifully

> Concerning this salvation, the prophets who prophesied about the grace that was to be yours searched and inquired carefully, inquiring what person or time the Spirit of Christ in them was indicating when he predicted the sufferings of Christ and the subsequent glories. It was revealed to them that they were serving not themselves but you, in the things that have now been announced to you through those who preached the good news to you by the Holy Spirit sent from heaven, things into which angels long to look.

The angels also were longing, the prophets were longing and now it has happened.

This is something that really excites me. In our country, if they bring in this anti-conversion law that they are trying to bring in, we don't know what will happen if we share the gospel. But this we know: our people need this message. This is what they are longing for but they don't know that it's what they are longing for.

● *Can you imagine not being free to speak to people about Christ? Pray for those parts of the world where sharing Christ can mean prison or death.*

In verse 10, Paul gives a little more about this mystery. He says it is 'a plan for the fullness of time, to unite all things in him, things in heaven and things on earth.' The NIV is very clear when reading but sometimes it changes the exact words, though it usually gives the right meaning. There's a word translated 'plan' in the ESV which is not in the NIV. It's the word 'stewardship.' This word was used for household management. It had the idea of 'This is the job that has been assigned to you.' But here it's used with the idea of a plan. God has a plan. Verse 10: 'a plan for the fullness of time, to unite all things in him, things in heaven and things on earth.' Right now we may be bewildered, we can't understand what's happening: but there's a plan.

Recently I was talking to an American missionary in Sri Lanka and he made me realise that God's plan encompasses my country. My country is in real trouble at the moment. You get very depressed and sometimes humiliated that you are so much for peace but peace doesn't seem to be going to work . . . but there's a plan. And in that plan Sri Lanka is also included. This is an exciting thought: we don't know the details of this plan but God has a plan for the universe. And this plan is to unite all things in him, things in heaven and things on earth.

We don't know exactly what this uniting involves; it certainly doesn't mean universal salvation – in other words that everyone is going to be saved – because this passage itself says that only some are going to receive God's salvation. Ephesians 2 talks about those who are outside of Christ being without hope and without God. So it doesn't mean that all will be saved. Philippians 2:10,11 talks about every knee bowing, every tongue confessing that Jesus is

Lord but that same statement (which is actually a quotation from Isaiah 45:23) is used in Romans 14:11 by Paul in connection with judgement. In other words, some who bow down, some who confess, are going to do so regretfully because they have rejected God and now it is too late.

In 1 Corinthians 15:28, Paul talks about God being 'all in all', which is very similar to saying he unites all. But before that, the enemies are going to be defeated and all things are going to be put in subjection under his feet (1 Cor. 15:24,25). So in the final victory, some are not going to be saved. Then what is happening? Obviously our knowledge is very sketchy. Paul is talking about what Revelation calls the new heaven and the new earth, where there will be no pain, no sorrow; the light of God's glory is going to reign in that place. His *shalom* or peace, about which we talked before, will be there. Creation is going to be redeemed. We are going to have a beautiful world and the saved people will be brought under the total joyous rule of Christ. We don't know the exact details but we do know that the world is going to be redeemed.

FURTHER STUDY

Psalm 51 is said to have been written by David after he had committed adultery with Bathsheba. It reveals David's humility – he knows he needs cleansing and a pure heart and admits it. He acknowledges before God that he needs forgiveness. What can we learn from David's attitude here?

REFLECTION AND RESPONSE

• 'I'm not a bad person. I try to be good. I've never murdered anyone.' This is a very common response to the whole issue of sin. But it's a deadly response. During this study there have been opportunities to pray for people who don't know Christ. They might not feel they need forgiveness; they might be involved in deceptive beliefs; they may think Christianity is nonsense; possibly, they are resisting the conviction of the Holy Spirit. Think about those you have already prayed for. Would it be appropriate to write, phone or visit? Write their names in the group journal and determine to keep praying for them.

• You may also wish to write down the names of Christian writers, novelists or dramatists whose work has blessed you or your family. How can you help or encourage those people? (If you don't know of any, look through a Christian magazine/browse your local Christian bookstore).

• Add to the journal the names of countries like Sri Lanka, where telling others about Christ can be very dangerous. Keep them in your prayers this week. Research what is going on around the world from organisations such as Jubilee Campaign or Open Doors.

• Thank God for his wonderful plans. We may not understand them but we can be sure they are good and perfect. Encourage one another to trust God with your own personal future, the future of your friends and family, your church and the wider world. Finish with a song declaring the Lordship of Christ.

CHAPTER 9

Truth and the Spirit

Aim: To examine the meaning of truth and the promise of the Holy Spirit

FOCUS ON THE THEME
Get into teams to play a game of *Call my Bluff*. Each person on the team must give a definition of a word. Only one must be the right definition. The others must be bluffs. Teams get a point for a successful bluff or for choosing the 'true' option first.

Read: Ephesians 1:7–10,13,14
Key verses: Ephesians 1:13,14

After describing the process of salvation, the way it begins and the way it ends, Paul describes what happens in between verses 13 and 14 now: 'In him you also, when you heard the word of truth, the gospel of your salvation and believed in him, were sealed with the promised Holy Spirit, who is the guarantee of our inheritance until we acquire possession of it to the praise of his glory.' We are told that the Holy Spirit is our guarantee. He also says a little about how we receive salvation. Verse 13 says 'you heard the word of truth, the gospel of your salvation and believed in him.'

THE WORD OF TRUTH

Let me just say a few words about the gospel being the word of truth. The value of truth has been greatly reduced in this post-modern generation. So much so, that to many if something feels good, it's okay, even if it's not true. That's why people say *The Da Vinci Code* is a lovely book even though it may not be historically accurate: it gives you a good feel.

● *'If it feels good, do it.' How can this belief wreck a life?*

Recently there was a big controversy over a person who was a recovered drug addict. He wrote his autobiography and it became very popular. Later it was discovered that some of the things this person said were not true. Others said, 'Even though it's not true, it's a very inspiring story and I think it's worth reading for that purpose.'

This is an example of how much truth is devalued by this post-modern generation. When people accept Christ, they accept Christ because he meets a need. Jesus is looked upon as the one who meets a need. Now let me say that yes, indeed, people accept Christ because he meets a need but they *stay* with Christ when they find that he's the truth. Others will accept Christianity because it's 'cool', it's the right thing for this time but when they find that their immediate needs are not met and the path of discipleship is a very costly path, they discover something else which is 'cool' for them. They say, 'We will embrace *this* for this stage of our lives.' They wouldn't do that if they understood the meaning of absolute truth, which is what the Bible talks about when it describes the truth of the gospel.

● *Today, people say: 'What's true for you isn't necessarily true for me.' But something is either true or it is not. How would you illustrate this fact?*

Earlier, I referred to Lindsay Brown's book about university students, *Shining like stars*.[17] In this book he refers to a girl called Amelia who was a university student in Peru. This was during the time when the Shining Path guerrillas were very powerful in the universities. This girl had become a Christian and the guerrillas' students had put up on the noticeboard a list of people whom they were going to kill because, in the eyes of the revolutionaries, they were reactionaries. One by one they began to kill these people and when the person was killed, that name would be cut off from the list on the noticeboard.

The Christians in the campus began to speak against this and they urged the revolutionaries not to do this. When that happened, the guerrillas said 'If you don't remain silent, we are going to kill you also.' Amelia got scared and said nothing about her new-found faith; she didn't talk about Christianity to anyone. For two years, she kept quiet. Then, she told Lindsay Brown, 'Six months ago, I asked a simple question: "Is the gospel true?" If it is true, it is worth living for and it is worth dying for.' She says, 'I had several months of reflection on this topic until I was finally convinced that Christianity is true. Since then, I've openly spoken about Christ, whatever it's going to cost me, because I know it's true.' She was willing to die because she knew it was true.

● *What would you have done in Amelia's situation?*

We are made with the capacity for appreciating truth. At the moment there are certain cultural factors involved in bringing this generation to think of objective truth as inferior and not essential. Such things often happen in history; cultural forces cause humans to downplay some aspect of what is important for complete humanness. Today it is truth that is under fire.

● *Think of a popular soap. Discuss the moral content and attitudes of individuals within the soap. Pick one or two who are embroiled in a situation that is not reflecting the truth of the gospel. How would you counsel these people from a godly perspective?*

I remember my professor in the early seventies, in theological college, J.T. Seamands, talking about communist China during the height of the Cultural Revolution under Mao Tse-Tung. Everyone was thinking of communism as the great enemy. Dr Seamands said, 'No culture can survive for very long without God. This is not going to last.' And how prophetic those words were. China became the scene where one of the greatest revivals in the history of the church took place.

That kind of thing can take place today too. People are made to appreciate truth and soon they will start looking for truth. Then where are they going to turn? When people in England realise that they need something more solid, more objective and reliable to put their trust in, where will they turn? Will they turn to the church and find that the church is so married to the culture that there is little about truth and a lot about experience? Will they turn to Islam and say, 'At least here there is something solid'? I hope that the church will be faithful in presenting the gospel, the message of truth.

● *What are some of the catalysts in life that might cause a person to look for something more 'solid'?*

● *Is your church a place where the uncompromising gospel is preached and lived out and the power of the Holy Spirit is in evidence?*

THE PROMISE OF THE SPIRIT

The seal

After belief, Paul says we are sealed with 'the promised Holy Spirit.' The Holy Spirit represents the fulfilment of the promises regarding the new covenant as found in Joel and Ezekiel (Joel 2:28–30; Ezek. 36:26,27). A seal was a very important thing in those days because many people couldn't read and write. The seal was an easily recognisable sign that indicated ownership. Usually it was a stamped imprint, bearing the seal of the owner, that was used to validate documents. For example, a will had to be presented to the authorities with the seal intact. The seal indicates ownership, it says 'This is authentic.' Paul says we are sealed with the Holy Spirit.

Having the Holy Spirit gives evidence that we are Christians. Experience *is* important to Christianity; it *is* part of the evidence for the reality of Christianity. It is not the only evidence but it is part of it. For example, in the house of Cornelius, Peter realised, 'These people are really Christians.' Why? 'They have received the Holy Spirit just as we received him.' So he was able to baptise them (Acts 10:45–48).

The experience of the Holy Spirit is like a seal which gives evidence that we are real Christians.

● *What is some of the evidence that a person has the Holy Spirit?*

The guarantee

Then Paul changes metaphors in the middle of the sentence and describes the Holy Spirit as 'the guarantee of our inheritance until we acquire possession of it' (v14). This word 'guarantee' comes three times in Paul's writings, referring to the work of the Holy Spirit. It's like a part-payment, the first instalment of what is going to be one day paid in full. It could be used of a ring that is given by a man to a woman as a pledge of his faithfulness to her. This is the idea that is found here. The Holy Spirit is a guarantee of our inheritance until we acquire possession of it in heaven.

How does the Spirit guarantee? How do we know that we'll go to heaven? One way of knowing is that Jesus is in our hearts through the Holy Spirit. We have experienced him.

I remember a famous preacher saying that he didn't like the song that says 'He lives, He lives, Christ Jesus lives in me.' What the preacher did not like was when the song said, 'You ask me how I know he lives? He lives within my heart.' He said that is not good reasoning because the evidence for Christianity is objective. Indeed, there is a lot of objective evidence for Christianity. But there is subjective evidence too. We have experienced Christ in our lives. We realise that we are indeed God's people because God is working in us. We have begun to taste the life of the future world. When an old man was asked whether he expected to get to heaven, he said, 'Why, I live there.' He had experienced God.

● *How have you experienced Christ in your own life this week?*

The structure of eschatology, of the future things, can be described as – 'Already and not yet.' We are already experiencing God but we have not yet come to the fullness of it. Fanny Crosby exemplified this in her life. When she was six weeks old, she had a slight cold and her eyes were inflamed. A doctor gave her the wrong medication and she went blind. She lived until she was ninety-five years old. She married a blind musician and had one child who died in infancy. She wrote more than eight thousand hymns. The overwhelming emotion of those hymns was joy.

When she was in her fifties, her friend Phoebe Palmer-Knapp composed a tune and brought it to her. And Fanny Crosby told Phoebe 'Play it for me.' She played it and said, 'What does the tune say?' She played it again and played it a third time and Fanny Crosby said, 'Blessed assurance, Jesus is mine, O what a foretaste of glory divine' and she wrote that song in a very short time.[18]

A minister once told Fanny Crosby that it was too bad that God did not give her the gift of sight. Fanny Crosby replied, 'If I had been given a choice at birth, I would have asked to be blind. For when I get to heaven, the first face I will see will be the face of the One who died for me.' Can you catch her sense of anticipation? Blessed assurance, Jesus is mine – but it's only a foretaste of glory divine.

We have received a guarantee and that guarantee is glorious. We have fallen in love with the Person who loved us and gave himself for us. And this love is only at the moment something like an engagement. One day there's going to be the marriage supper of the Lamb, when this relationship is going to be consummated.

The past is forgiven and forgotten; the future is glorious. And now, in the present, we have a foretaste of God's glory.

FURTHER STUDY

Look at John 3:1–21; John 14:16,17,25; John 16: 7–15. What do we learn in these passages about the work of the Spirit in conversion and conviction? Note that he is called the Spirit of truth.

REFLECTION AND RESPONSE

• Pilate said, 'What is truth?' Spend some time reflecting on your life. Are there any areas where truth might be compromised? What can you do about it?

• Relating our own true experiences of Christ's presence is important when witnessing to unbelievers. Think of a time when Jesus has been very real to you or that he has touched you in a special way. Commit your feelings about this to paper, either written or drawn. You may like to make an individual or group collage using pictures from magazines as a background for your words or to illustrate your experience.

- Think about people who may be looking for truth but dismiss the church because they do not believe established religion, as they perceive it, can provide an answer. Brainstorm ideas about how you can bring 'church' to them: e.g. seasonal involvement, events for children, community projects, social events – picnics, barbecues, treasure hunts, walks – starting a community Prayer Service and so on. Resolve to make at least one of your ideas a reality.

- Invite people to add anything they wish to the group journal, then pray together: 'O God our Father, thank you for Jesus who is the Way, the Truth and the Life. Thank you that the past is forgotten in the sea of God's forgetfulness. And thank you, Lord, that here on earth we have been given a glimpse of the glory that awaits us in the future. We pray that you will help us to be faithful now, so that we will take many others with us to heaven. In Jesus' name we pray. Amen.'

REVIEW OF EPHESIANS 1:7–10,13,14:
We have discovered some very deep theology in these verses. We have covered redemption, atonement, seeing our need, truth and the seal, guarantee and experience of the Holy Spirit. What has challenged you most? Talk about it with the group and add to the group journal.

POINTS TO PONDER
- What have you learned about God?

- What have you learned about yourself?

- What actions or attitudes do you need to change as a result?

CHAPTER 10

Being thankful

Aim: To grasp the importance of thankfulness

FOCUS ON THE THEME
Think of five things you are grateful for. Then think of five people you are grateful for. Praise God for his goodness.

Read: Ephesians 1:15–18a
Key verses: Ephesians 1:15,16

We have just finished the long sentence of twelve verses: 202 words of Paul's eulogy. Now after that he has another long sentence, nine verses long. It's about his prayer for the Ephesians. A eulogy was unusual at the start of a letter, but the prayer is usual. As is often the case in Paul's letters, it starts with a thanksgiving and then goes on to an intercessory prayer. In ten of his thirteen letters, Paul mentions praying for the people to whom he's writing.

THANKING GOD

Paul starts his prayer with thanksgiving: 'For this reason, because I have heard of your faith in the Lord Jesus and your love toward all the saints, I do not cease to give thanks to you, remembering you in my prayers, that the God of our Lord Jesus Christ, the Father of glory, may give you a spirit of wisdom and of revelation in the knowledge of him . . . ' (vv15,16a). He says 'for this reason' he had been describing great truths about God and then, he says, 'because of these great truths, now I am going to thank God for you.' In other words, these great truths that he had just celebrated have become real in the lives of the Ephesians. After this profound and exalted theology, he could thank God for the way it was applied in the lives of these people.

It's not at all unnatural to find Paul criss-crossing in his writings between high theology and the situation in individuals' lives. This is because all theology is practical theology. To make a strict distinction between systematic or dogmatic theology and practical theology is not a biblical practice. All theology is practical and everything we do comes out of theology.

Paul says, 'I have heard of your faith.' It's about five to seven years since Paul has visited Ephesus. Now he has got news about them and he gives thanks to God for that news. In verses 3 to 14 there is praise for gospel truths; and verses 15 and 16 are thanks to God for how the gospel influenced people. We glorify God for who he is and what he has done and thank God for what other people do. Then we intercede for these people.

This is a good combination to maintain in our prayer and devotional time. We develop a system whereby we can praise God for who he is and what he has done, thank God for what he has done in people and then pray to God for people. You see all of these elements in this prayer. Each one of us needs to develop a devotional pattern that is appropriate for us. My system is to separate a day for praise during my devotional time; I do that once in every five, six, seven or eight days. That day, I spend most of my prayer time singing hymns and praising God. Then almost every day, I have times of thanking God and interceding for people. Make sure that there is praise and thanks and intercession in your prayer time.

- *Think about your own prayer life. Do you have a pattern? Do you need to develop one?*
- *What part does praise play in your Quiet Time? Determine to spend some time each day this week praising God for who he is and what he has done.*

WITH A GRATEFUL HEART . . .

Paul even thanks God for the Corinthians, in 1 Corinthians, where we see that he has so many problems with them. In 1 Corinthians 1:4 he says, 'I give thanks to my God always' – he's always thanking God for these Corinthians who are giving him so many problems. Why does he thank God? 'Because of the grace of God that was given to us in Christ Jesus.' God's grace is available to them. Paul had learned the discipline of looking at people through the eyes of grace.

- *Do you look at people through the eyes of grace? If not, how might looking at people in this way change your attitude towards your Christian and non-Christian family, friends and colleagues?*

There are many places in his letters where Paul praises people and tells the good things that they have done because of what God has done in their lives. Barnabas went to the new church in Antioch, and there would have been a lot of weaknesses in the church there. But Acts 11:23 tells us that he saw the grace of God and he was gladdened by the sight of these believers. David says in Psalm 16:3: 'As for the saints of the land, they are the excellent ones in whom is all my delight.' He delights in fellow believers.

There are some unhappy Christians who are always finding fault with people and speaking ill of others. They never give the other person the benefit of the doubt. Other Christians need to spend much time and energy trying to remove their anger and hurt. I spent a long time talking to my wife this morning and praying with her because somebody in our church has got very hurt over something that happened and we were wondering how to respond to this particular hurt. The dominant approach to life and people that these people have is 'people are bad.' And because of that they always see bad in people. That's not the biblical lifestyle. The biblical lifestyle says that where sin abounds, grace super-abounds. If you are overwhelmed by grace, if you are thrilled by grace, you recognise grace in another person. And this recognising of grace in others is one of the keys to joy in our lives.

A Christian named John Miller says 'How happy a person is depends upon the depth of his gratitude.' That's the way a person can be happy. Take the case of a married couple: there are so many weaknesses in both the husband and the wife. Some of those weaknesses are not going to change till we go to heaven, however much we try to change them. You can choose to harp on these weaknesses or you can choose to celebrate the many good points that this person has. When the other person knows that you celebrate those good points, then they will be joyous. And when your family life is joyous, your home becomes a joyous place.

- *Are you a fault-finder? Remind yourself of Jesus' words in Matthew 7:1–5, Luke 6:41,42. What steps do you need to take to stop finding fault in others this week?*
- *Do you have an attitude of gratitude? How can you begin to live a thankful lifestyle?*
- *Is there someone you are trying to change? Ask God to help you be more accepting and to concentrate on their good points. (Is there someone you need to apologise to?)*

I'm not talking about naïve, positive thinking. When Paul found reports of serious sin and false teaching in the churches, he thundered angrily. He had such a zeal for God that when God was dishonoured, he was angry. And he also had such a zeal for God that when God was honoured, he was joyful and thanked God. So thanksgiving was very prominent in his life. He says, in this passage, 'I do not cease to give thanks.' It happened all the time. Let's look at what he thanked God for.

FOR FAITH

First he thanks God for their 'faith in the Lord Jesus.' In verse 1 he describes them as faithful in Christ Jesus. These are believers in Christ and now everything is influenced by that belief in Jesus. Faith is the key to their lives. We don't have to be great people to exercise great faith, because what matters is not our great faith but our faith in a great God. That's the key to greatness, faith in a great God – he's the One who's great. I read somewhere that Hudson Taylor worked hard at trying to develop his faith, until he stopped looking at his faith and learned to rest in the Faithful One.

● *Spend a few moments thinking about the greatness of our awesome, faithful God, in whom we can have complete confidence. How would you answer someone who said 'I've got faith' but didn't seem sure in what or whom they had faith?*

● *Are you working hard to develop your faith? Stop. God doesn't want us to strive in this way. He wants us to rest in him. How can you begin to do that this week?*

Mark 11:22, 'Have faith in God' became the great theme in Hudson Taylor's life. He translated this as 'Hold God's faithfulness.' He regarded this as a creed for his life. He once said, 'All God's giants have been weak men who did great things for God because they reckoned on God being with them.' That is the key to greatness in the Christian life; believing that God is with us. May we be known as people whose vision of God directs all that we do. When pain and heartache come to us, we say, 'God will look after me.' That's faith. When we have an obstacle, we say, 'God will see me through.' We will be severely tempted to compromise. For example, when somebody says bad stories about us and we want to expose that person and tell the truth in a way that will hurt that person who has hurt us: at such times, we say, 'God will defend me. I don't need to hurt the people who hurt me.' When we have a strong temptation to take revenge on a person who humiliates us, we say, 'God will honour me in his time. I'll wait for God to do that for me.' That's faith: believing that God is able to look after us.

● *'God will look after me; he will see me through; he will defend me so I don't need to get my revenge.' How true is this response for you, when your life hits a crisis point, you are under pressure or under attack?*

Hudson Taylor once said, 'God's work done in God's way will never lack God's supply.' We trust in God, we follow his principles, believing that he will see us through. The Ephesians had faith.

FURTHER STUDY
Read Psalm 100. This is a short psalm of worship, thanks and praise to the faithful God to whom we belong. Note the use of words like 'joy' and 'gladness.' What does the psalmist encourage people to do in verse 2? For what reason should we give thanks to God (v5)? Look at other psalms of praise and thanksgiving. Perhaps you could incorporate them into your times of prayer this week.

REFLECTION AND RESPONSE

- Reflect on today's theme of thanksgiving. Think of one of the people you thanked God for when you were focusing on the theme. Can you see God working in their lives? Give thanks to him for what he is doing.

- 'All theology is practical and everything we do comes out of theology.' How is this truth affecting your life as you continue through this study book?

- Spend time thanking God as a group for what God is doing in your lives and in the lives of other Christians known to you. You may like to share about salvation, growth or healing or good news of what God is doing in any organisations you pray for or that your church works with.

- Finish with a song of praise and thanksgiving.

Time to love

Aim: To be challenged to love others practically and in prayer

FOCUS ON THE THEME
Love. What's your first thought? Go round the group for quick-fire answers. Then think of a love story you have read or watched lately (perhaps one that has just been mentioned). How was that love portrayed? The world's idea of 'love' is often the sentimental, romantic or sexual kind. Talk together about other types of love . . . the types that aren't portrayed in films.

Read: Ephesians 1:15–18a
Key verses: Ephesians 1:15–18a

Next we are told the Ephesians had 'love towards all the saints' (v15b). Paul mentions love in five of his thanksgivings. In four, he mentions love for the saints and in three he mentions love for all the saints.

LOVE IN DIFFICULTY

Can we love all Christians? Don't we dislike some Christians? What unites us is greater than what divides us. We have spiritual and theological reasons to love Christians. Chapter 4:1–16 expounds the reasons why we can love these people. We belong to the same body and share the most important things in life in common with these people.

There may be emotional reasons that make it difficult for us to love some people: their personalities may have features that we don't like. There may be experiential reasons for not liking them. But our devotion to Christ is not based on emotions, personality and experience. It's based on spiritual and theological reasons. And these things are the things that are most important to us.

● *Is there a Christian you don't like? Examine why you don't like that person. Is it just a matter of temperamental differences? Or have they hurt you in some way? Ask Jesus to show his love for that person in and through you this week. How can you begin to take practical steps to get along with them?*

Therefore, out of devotion to Christ and out of an understanding of Christianity, we love all Christians. This is Christian love; the characteristic word used for Christian love is *agape*. It was not a very common word in those days but it seems that the early church used it because it helped people understand what Christian love was all about. *Agape* love is decisive love. It doesn't just happen; we make it happen.

People fall in love . . . it's something that happens that you can't avoid. It happens automatically – no effort is involved in falling in love. In Christianity, you decide to love the unlovable. However difficult it may be, we love them because that is part of obedience to the command of Jesus.

Twice during the Last Supper, Jesus said, 'Love one another as I have loved you' (Jn. 13:34; 15:12) and the context there is giving one's life for one's friends. Christian love is active; it expresses itself in the service of others.

LOVE IN SERVICE

Acts chapters 2 and 4 say that the Christians shared everything. No-one was in need, because these Christians considered what they owned as not theirs any more. What we own is not ours, it belongs to God and all of us belong to God. John says, 'If anyone has the world's goods and sees his brother in need, yet closes his heart against him, how does God's love abide in him?' Christians are always changing their plans because of the needs of others (1 Jn. 3:17).

● *On a scale of one to ten, how irritated do you get when your personal plans are interrupted by someone else's needs? What can you do to more lovingly accommodate the needs of others this week?*

I think one of the most dangerous aspects of contemporary worldliness is that people are not ashamed of selfishness any more. Selfish ambition is considered something to be proud of. Selfishness has become decent today. But selfish ambition destines people to unhappiness.

● *'Those who live for others are happier than those who live for themselves.' Do you agree or disagree? Can you think of someone who has lived solely for themselves but seems happy? Would you swap places with them? Why/why not?*

Christians can't have perfectly planned lives because the needs of others crop up at the most inconvenient times. Dietrich Bonhoeffer has some wise words to say about this

We must allow ourselves to be interrupted by God. God will be constantly crossing our paths and cancelling our plans by sending us people with claims and petitions. We may pass them by, preoccupied with our more important tasks, as the priest passed by the man who had fallen among thieves, perhaps reading the Bible. When we do that we pass by the visible sign of the Cross raised athwart our path to show us that, not our way, but God's way must be done. It is a strange fact that Christians and even ministers frequently consider their work so important and urgent that they will allow nothing to disturb them. They think that they are doing God a service in this, but actually they are disdaining God's 'crooked yet straight' path (Gottfried Arnold). They do not want a life that is crossed and baulked. But it is part of the discipline of humility that we must not spare our hand where it can perform a service and that we do not assume that our schedule is our own to manage, but allow it to be arranged by God.[19]

● *Is there anyone you need to make time for?*

I read a very exciting book some months ago by Rodney Stark, who is a sociologist, called *The Rise of Christianity*. It explains how the Christian church, which was a small entity in the Roman Empire, conquered the whole Empire within three centuries. He has different chapters giving reasons why this happened.[20]

One chapter was on epidemics. He says that two major epidemics hit the Roman Empire during those first three centuries. Many, many people died. If they had been looked after, their lives might have been saved. But when some of them got sick, their relatives left them because they were afraid of contracting the disease themselves. It was found that during this epidemic the percentages of Christians who lived after having got sick were much higher than those who were not Christians. This is because Christians didn't abandon their sick relatives. Not only that, Christians cared for others who had been abandoned and helped save their lives. Rodney Stark says that this was one of the factors that contributed to the fast growth of Christianity during the first three centuries of the church.

Today, people fiercely protect their privacy and yet are left thirsting for community. The Christian community will fill that need. Of course we are afraid of hurt, because when you get close to people you can be sure that you are going to be hurt. Yet the joy of the Lord gives us strength to face that hurt. People will hurt us. And they will keep hurting us. But God gives us strength and our fulfilment comes from God, not from our service or from people. And when people hurt us, we run to God and cling to him and his love pours in as we cling to him. Our pain is tinged with the glow of God's love. In the midst of the pain, therefore, there is a deep joy because we have been loved by God. In fact, the pain becomes an occasion for us to experience the depth of God's joy in a new way. So we love people, however much it may hurt us.

● *Are you a 'private person'? Does the thought of getting too close to people scare you? Reflect quietly and share thoughts if you would like to.*

LOVE IN PRAYER

Notice the two things that Paul thanks God for – faith and love. Are these the most important things in our lives? Are these the most important things that come to our minds when we think about people? Today, if you hear a testimony or a prayer request, most of them have to do with temporal, material needs – a job, health, housing, provision of funds and things like that. You might find a mother who has a son who is full of faith and love. But he's not a very good student or maybe doesn't have a good job or has not been able to find a partner to get married. Very often the predominant feeling of that mother about that son is one of disappointment. That is worldliness: there are such wonderful things about this son, but the mother is disappointed.

● *Sometimes we over-value achievement or status. How do you define success?*
● *Do you feel that acceptance in your church is in any way performance-related? How can you help all the people in the congregation feel loved and accepted – even if they can't 'do' as much as others, for whatever reason?*

Some Youth for Christ workers serve in dangerous places and sometimes, when war is raging, I get very worried about them. But when I pray for them, the most important thing I pray for is 'Oh God, make them saints.' Because if they are saints, however difficult the situation is, they will be able to be God's people and experience God's protection.

So Paul thanks God for them. Then he intercedes for them (v 16–18). He says he remembers them in his prayers. This was Paul's regular practice: in ten of his thirteen letters, he says that he prays for the recipients. For Timothy, who was his spiritual child, he prayed night and day (2 Tim. 1:3). I don't know how Paul remembered to pray for all the people he prayed for. But to remember today, I think we will need some aids. Spurgeon, in his sermon on this same passage, talks about how we can use a prayer list to help us to remember. I use photographs; my room is full of photographs, arranged in different categories such as family, ministry, church, leaders, scholars and friends. I use these photos to help me to pray. Because I can't take the photographs when I travel, I have a prayer list in my diary for my travel purposes, with the names written down. In my diary, I put down important events in people's lives. For example, if somebody has an exam at three o'clock today, I will write 'Three o'clock, so-and-so's exam' so that I can remember to pray. I keep changing and modifying the techniques. Why? Because this is the most important thing I do. And if it's the most important thing I do, I must use the best methods possible to do this work. Learn to look at prayer with the interest of a professional.

Is prayer really the most important thing we do? James 5:16 says: 'The prayer of a righteous person has great power as it is working.' Praying for people is one of the most powerful things that we can do.

● *What aids can you use to remember others in prayer? Here are some ideas but brainstorm others:*
  – *Photos – pin photos on a board or make a special Prayer Album with different categories (e.g. family/friends, church leaders, missionaries, the sick, your country/world issues, etc.)*
  – *Make a list – or a series of short lists for different days. One long list can seem very daunting.*
  – *Diary – or Prayer Calendar. Make a note of different people/issues for different weeks or days. Don't forget to mark days for special prayer opportunities or requests such as exams/hospital appointments.*
  – *Which do you think would be the best for you?*

There was man called John Scudder who first came to Sri Lanka and then he went to South India as a missionary. He had eight children and all of them became missionaries. The granddaughter of John Scudder was one of the great missionaries to India: Ida Scudder. She founded one of the most respected hospitals and medical schools in South Asia, the Christian medical college and hospital in Vellore, India. John Scudder says that those eight children were literally prayed into the kingdom by their mother. The mother used to spend the birthday of a child fasting and praying for that child. In 1 Samuel 12:23, Samuel, as the leader of the people, says, '. . . as for me, far be it from me if I should sin against the Lord by ceasing to pray for you.' W.E. Sangster says, 'As we mature in prayer, we'll find that we spend more time in intercession than in the other segments of prayer.'

Henry Martin is one of the most heroic figures that your country produced. He was one of the best students in mathematics at Cambridge, receiving the Wrangler award. But he didn't go into any of the wonderful jobs that were available for him. He went as a missionary to India and then to Iran to work among the Muslims. We often quote a statement from him: 'Let me burn out for God.' We forget the context of that statement. Listen to what he says after making that statement: 'Let me burn out for God. After all, whatever God may appoint, prayer is the great thing. Oh, that I might be a man of prayer.'

Please don't say that you don't have time to pray. If you don't have time, make time. It's the most important thing. People don't say they don't have time to eat. They make time to eat. If you are too busy to pray, you're too busy. Something has to change. Prayer will help you to become more efficient with your time. When you stop to be with God each day, you receive his power, you become in tune with God, so that you're flowing in the direction in which God is taking you for your life; your mind gets cleared as you spend time alone with him. It slows you down so that you can think clearly. And all of these things combine to help us to work better.

● *Do you feel you are in tune with God, flowing in the direction he is taking you for your life? If not, how can you spend some valuable time with him this week?*

There's a beautiful book written by Robert Coleman, called *The Mind of the Master*.[21] He refers to Mark 6:31 where we are told that Jesus had so many people coming to see him that he had no time to eat. Then Coleman refers to verse 46 which says that he went alone and spent time in prayer. Dr Coleman says 'He could get along without food but he could not live without prayer.' And then he says, 'He never got behind in his work because he never got behind in prayer.' Let's find time to pray for people.

● *How does the fact that Jesus got along without food but couldn't get along without prayer speak to you?*

FURTHER STUDY
Read John 13:1–16; John 14:15,23,24; John 15:9–17. How does Jesus' example of service and command to love challenge you today?

REFLECTION AND RESPONSE
- As a group, think of any ways you can show your love for each other in practical service this week (shopping, DIY, babysitting, gardening, giving lifts etc.) You may also like to pick a group project, such as a country/troubled area/missionary venture that is known to you. Commit to intercessory prayer for this and for each other.

- Write out the words of 1 Corinthians 13:13 and put them inside your purse or wallet. Every time you see them, remember that Jesus loves you and every person you meet – at the check-out, in the bank, working, busking or begging . . . and that his values are not the world's values.

- Close by praying that you will be able to 'slow down' and seek God this week. Note any thoughts on the theme of love in the group journal.

CHAPTER 12

Knowing God

Aim: To encourage us to want to know God better

FOCUS ON THE THEME
Imagine your group is holding a dinner party with a difference. You can invite anyone you like – rich, famous, dead or alive – but they have to be people you have never met in the flesh. Make up your own 'fantasy guest' list and talk about why you would invite those people.

Read: Ephesians 1:15–18a
Key verses: Ephesians 1:17,18a

SEEING HIS GLORY

There is something very interesting about the way Paul prays. He says he prays to 'the God of our Lord Jesus Christ, the Father of glory.' In our efficiency-oriented world, we simply say 'Father' or 'God' or something like that and get on with the business of praying for something. For Paul, it was important when he prayed to remember whom he was praying to, to give God his worth. Or as the Old Testament puts it, 'To ascribe to God' or, as Revelation puts it, 'You are worthy to receive honour.' In the Bible, prayers to God are often prefaced with a description of God. These are all aspects of Christian meditation. Sometimes this becomes verbose, long-winded and superficial. That's when it's done for effect. But if it's done out of adoration, it helps us focus on God and it brings honour to God.

Sometimes I use an Armenian prayer book for my devotions (Armenian as in the ethnic group). It has prayers written by St Gregory of Narek who is the patron saint of the Armenian people. In this prayer book you find line after line, affirmation after affirmation, where he tells who God is. It's tremendously edifying to be able to do that, to stop from our busy activity and to focus on God. Here's an example: 'Lord, O Lord, who bears no grudges, tolerant, forgiving, compassionate, powerful and merciful, behold your actions rest on truth, your judgement upon confessions, your decisions upon sound testimony, O Seer of the unseen.' What happens when I read Gregory's prayers is that I stop what I am doing to meditate on who God is. It is a way of honouring God.

● *In your prayers this week, try to spend the first part adoring God. You may wish to use a prayer book (ancient or modern), read a psalm (such as Psalm 96) or read/sing a song that ascribes greatness to our awesome Creator. How does spending time in adoration change the rest of your prayer-life?*

So Paul says 'the God of our Lord Jesus Christ, the Father of glory.' The NIV says 'glorious Father' which is possibly too weak. What he's saying is, 'You're the Father of glory.' Peter O'Brien says the idea here is that God is the source of all true glory. Generally when we use 'glory', we're talking about the splendour, the brightness of the divine presence – what was called *shekinah* in the Old Testament, when the glory came down to the tabernacle and to the Temple. Today, our *shekinah* is when Jesus came down from heaven and tabernacled among us and lived and died and rose again and ascended to heaven. So that is our vision of glory, as we think of the glory of God in the face of the Lord Jesus Christ.

● *Meditate on what it means to see the glory of God in the face*
   of Christ. How is he described in Hebrews 1:3? And how
   does this reflection influence you to respond to Jesus in
   prayer and worship?

KNOWING GOD MORE

Paul's prayer is essentially that the Ephesians may increase
in the knowledge of God (v17). He prays that 'the Father of
glory may give you a spirit of wisdom and of revelation in
the knowledge of him . . . ' (v17b). As we grow in the
knowledge of God, we grow as Christians because we
begin to realise our riches in Christ: the vision of God's
glory transforms us as people. Paul says, 'And we all, with
unveiled face, beholding the glory of the Lord . . . ' If we
behold the glory of the Lord, then what happens? We 'are
being transformed into the same image from one degree of
glory to another' (2. Cor. 3:18).

   When I first got married to my wife, I used to laugh at
some of the expressions her family used. I thought these
were odd. Now, after thirty years of marriage, I find that
I'm using the same expressions – things that I laughed at.
When you stay close to somebody, that person's nature
becomes one with you.

● *Think of someone you know well. Can you see how that*
   person's nature has affected your own and vice versa, even
   down to little mannerisms or quirks of speech? Does this
   encourage you to spend more time with God?

One of the most amazing chapters in the Bible is in
Numbers, where we see the reaction of Moses, when his
brother and sister rebelled against him and began to
question his authority. To me, the most amazing verse in

that whole chapter (Num. 12) is when his sister, Miriam, is hit with leprosy. The Hebrew there is very strong. It suggests an urgent outburst. 'And Moses cried to the Lord, "Oh God, please heal her – please"' (Num. 12:13). This woman has been rebelling against him and God has punished her and he cries out to God to heal her.

Earlier on in that same chapter, we are told that Moses was the meekest man in the world. How was he able to do this? Moses had seen the glory of God. Often, when he went up to be with God and saw the glory of God, he was lifted to a level of exaltation – in other words, humility. For the Christian, to be exalted is to be humble. He had been lifted to such a level that it influenced the way he thought and acted. Revenge, pride, self-seeking was now below his dignity. He had become glorious, just like God is glorious. So Paul prays that they may see the glory of God, the riches of God and through that, become new people. When we see God, we change automatically.

● *'For the Christian, to be exalted is to be humble.' How easy do we find it to live in humility?*

It is possible for a Christian not to see the glory of God. When I was writing this down, a member of our church called me. She's a dear old lady, a devoted Christian but she was having all sorts of problems and was depressed. After she had talked, I said, 'God will look after you.' She said, 'God has left me. He's not looking after me. He looks after others but he's not looking after me.' She was suffering because her vision had been blocked. The suffering was now causing her to feel that God was not with her, whereas actually suffering could be a means by which we get closer to God.

● *When is it easy to believe God has left us? Do you know of anyone who might believe that right now? Pray for them.*

In Philippians 3:10, Paul expresses a great desire to know God and says that the way he will know God is by experiencing the power of the resurrection and by sharing in Christ's sufferings, becoming like him in his death.

Oswald Sanders has written a beautiful book called *Enjoying Intimacy with God*. There he talks about a godly woman he knew who was dying of cancer. She knew she had only a few days to live and because of that, her husband was attending to her every need, trying to make things as easy as possible for her. And she told the husband, 'You must not make things too easy for me. I must keep growing, you know.' Here she is, ready to die and she wants to grow. Every experience is viewed from the perspective of wanting to know God more. Philippians 3:8: 'Indeed, I count everything as loss because of the surpassing worth of knowing Christ Jesus my Lord. For his sake I have suffered the loss of all things and I count them as rubbish, in order that I may gain Christ . . . '

John Stam and his wife Betty were killed by the communists in China in 1934. He was twenty-seven-years old and she was twenty-eight. John Stam said: 'Take away everything I have but do not take away the sweetness of walking and talking with the King of glory.' We want to know God more. That is the greatest thing about life.

● *Since meeting Jesus, do you find that things you thought important before now seem worthless, compared to knowing him?*

WISDOM AND REVELATION

Paul says that we know God through two ways – by 'a spirit of wisdom and of revelation in the knowledge of him' (v.17). This is not automatic. We are to pray that we will get it.

That's why Paul says, 'I pray that you will get to know God more.' So how does God show us himself? What are the things that God uses to give us a greater knowledge of him?

I think times of crisis are among the best things to know God – afflictions. Martin Luther said that affliction was the best book in his library. The best way to learn is through afflictions. Why? Because you go to God like a child and say, 'Oh God, I need you, I need your help.' As Richard Halverson says, 'The growing edge of the Christian life is need.' When we are needy, we become open to finding out more about God. Stanley Jones once said, 'All my life I carried a cross and now that cross has been taken away and now I'm praying for another cross because that cross has made me what I am.' That is the attitude of one who is receptive to God, looking at life through the eyes of faith.

● *Find a stone or small rock. Paint on it the word 'Strength.'*
  Place it on your desk or on a windowsill, where you will see
  it often. Let it remind you that God is our Rock, our
  Strength in times of crisis. Who else could you paint a
  'strength stone' for?

Wisdom and revelation come through lingering in the presence of God so that we can orient our thoughts towards God's thoughts. We need to linger with God in prayer and the word. We must listen to the teaching of the word.

The book by Sam Gordon on Ephesians that I mentioned before talks about a famous preacher called Harry Ironside who, early in his ministry, met a godly old man called Andrew Foster who was dying of tuberculosis. One day after a long conversation with Andrew Foster, Harry Ironside asked him, 'Andrew, how come you know God so well? Where did you acquire your depth of knowledge of God and his word?' Andrew replied, 'I learned these things on my knees, on the mud floor of a little thatched house in the north of Ireland. There, with my Bible open before me, I used to kneel for hours at a time and ask the Spirit of God to reveal Christ to my soul and to open the word to my heart. He taught me more on my knees on that mud floor than I ever could have learned in all the seminaries and colleges in the world.' So, plan times to be with God, daily and sometimes just as a feast, to have a little extra time of communion with God.

Then Paul prays in verse 18 that they might have 'the eyes of their hearts enlightened.' The heart is the seat of thoughts, emotions and volition. What we do and what we think comes because of the way our hearts are. So he's talking about having spiritual eyesight. That's how F.F. Bruce translates it – 'May your spiritual eyesight be enlightened.' The Holy Spirit brings light to our darkened hearts, so that we would see things as they really are. 2 Corinthians 4:18 says 'we look not to the things that are seen but to the things that are unseen; for the things that are seen are transient but the things that are unseen are eternal.' God needs to open our eyes so that we can see these things. We have to be receptive to God. In 2 Timothy 2:7, Paul says, 'Think over what I say, for the Lord will give you understanding in everything.' We have to think and God gives us understanding.

The life of faith is a life where we open ourselves to God every day so that he can keep teaching us.

● *Last time, we spoke of the importance of slowing down. Remember that when we slow down, we can become more in tune with God and can think more clearly. We also receive his power. Have you managed to slow down and be with God more?*

These people had faith and love for all the saints, but they needed to grow even more in their understanding of God's ways. The journey of discovery is something that will go on until we die. That's why we don't have to be bored even when we retire and don't have much to do. We can still spend time with God. We can still read the word. My mother is a lover of the Bible but now she can't see well enough to read so she has got audio CDs of the Bible. Very often when I go to her house she's listening to the Scriptures.

● *Sometimes, retired people can feel isolated or not useful to the church, through illness or immobility. Think of some older Christians you know. How can you help them to (a) be involved in the life of the church (b) feel they are still of worth to the Christian community (c) keep growing in God?*

We can always get more knowledge about God. God's truth is so vast that we could never plumb its depths or scale its heights. A person called Justus Jonas told Martin Luther, 'There is in Holy Scripture a wisdom so profound that no man may thoroughly study it or comprehend it.' Luther responded, 'Aye; we must ever remain scholars [or students] here. We cannot sound the depths of a single verse in Scripture. We get hold of but the ABC [of that verse] and that imperfectly.'[22]

I hope that your life will be characterised by faith and love and every day you will be trying to plumb the depths of God's truth. As you do that, I hope you experience some of the joy that comes of knowing about the one who loves you so much that he died for you. Happy learning.

FURTHER STUDY

'. . . Moses was a very humble man, more humble than anyone else on the face of the earth' (Num. 12:3, NIV). Do you think he was always humble? Brought up in Pharaoh's palace, murdering the Egyptian, giving five excuses when he didn't want to obey God . . .

This week, read through Exodus 2:11 – 4:17. Let the story of Moses' earlier life and attitude encourage you that as you get closer to God and see his glory, he will change you too.

REFLECTION AND RESPONSE

- Think about what it means 'to know' someone. In the guest list from Focus on the theme, you chose people you have never met. You may have read about them, heard others talk about them – perhaps you 'know all about' them. How much of your relationship with God can be said to be 'knowing about' rather than 'knowing'? Spend some time in thoughtful reflection.

- In pairs, look at Philippians 3:7–11. Can you identify with Paul's own desires? Do you really want to know God more? How can you be even more open to God every day, so that you might be further changed by being in the glory of his presence?

- If you know of anyone who is having a particularly bad time, pray for them now. If one of the group is going through a period of crisis, encourage them with what you have learned today.

- Pray together: 'Father, we pray that you will give us a hunger, a thirst, for you, so that we may express that thirst in our reactions to people, in our reactions to problems and in our scheduling of our time so that we can grow in our knowledge of you. We do so want to know you better. In Jesus' name we pray. Amen.'

REVIEW OF EPHESIANS 1:15–18A:

In these few verses, we have learned an enormous amount about thankfulness, gratitude, faith, love, prayer, seeing God's glory and knowing him better. Pray together: 'Father, thank you for who you are and for all that you have done for us. Thank you for the gift of your precious Son. Help us to always have an "attitude of gratitude" and to love each other as you first loved us. Lord, help us to know you better and to show your love in our daily lives. Amen.'

POINTS TO PONDER
• What have you learned about God?

• What have you learned about yourself?

• What actions or attitudes do you need to change as a result?

CHAPTER 13

Hope and riches

Aim: To explore the meaning of Christian hope and true riches

FOCUS ON THE THEME
Entrepreneur Ray Rich has a huge house, several smart cars and his girlfriend is a model. He believes in himself, not God; he thinks when you're dead, you're dead. Harry Hopeful, on the other hand, is in jail. He has no worldly goods and his wife has gone off with another man. But he's become a Christian and wants to live the rest of his life (inside or out) with his eyes on his future reward in Christ. Imagine or role-play a conversation between these two characters. Who has the real hope? And who has the real riches?

Read: Ephesians 1:18–23
Key verse: Ephesians 1:18

We have seen how Paul had prayed that the hearts of the people would be enlightened so that they would know God more. After having said that, he tells of what he wishes for them to find out about God. Christians don't necessarily experience this automatically and so it was necessary for Paul to remind them of the things that he wants them to know about God.

He says '. . . that you may know what is the hope to which he has called you, what are the riches of his glorious inheritance in the saints, and what is the immeasurable greatness of his power toward us who believe' (Eph.1:18). There are three things that he wants them to know.

THE HOPE OF OUR CALLING

The first is 'the hope to which he has called [us].' Let me say a few words about the importance of hope in the New Testament. Hope completes the familiar biblical triad. Earlier Paul had spoken about their faith and their love and it is completed by hope. We said earlier that we have a 'Now and not yet' approach to life. We experience something of the glory of Christianity now. Yet that is only a foretaste – we hope for the completion of this.

Leon Morris complains that hope has been downgraded among Christians from blazing certainty to feeble optimism. Hope was very important to Paul. The noun appears thirty-six times in his writings and the verb nineteen times: a total of fifty-five times. It comes in all his letters except 2 Timothy, which of course talks beautifully about the hope that he has of going to heaven and receiving the crown of righteousness (2 Tim. 4:6–8).

We must remember always that we haven't received all our blessings but that we are confident that we will receive them. Paul talks in 1 Corinthians 15 about why we are so confident. His whole argument there is based on what he sees as our solidarity with Christ. We are one body, Christ is the Head and if the Head rose from the dead, then the body also will rise. What happened to Christ is going to happen to us. He argues powerfully that we are people who are living this side of Christ's resurrection, which is going to result in our experiencing resurrection too.

In Ephesians 1:18 Paul describes hope as 'the hope to which he has called you.' When God called us, along with that call came certain things that we are to hope for. Let's look at some of these things that are part of our salvation, which we haven't yet experienced.

Eternal life – true, eternal life is primarily a quality that we experience now; but it also has a temporal aspect. It's going to last for ever and ever. We are called to eternal life (Titus 1:2 and 3:7). Then we have the hope of sharing his glory (Col. 1:27): '. . . Christ in you, the hope of glory.' This includes *resurrection to an incorruptible body*. We are going to have a wonderful body without all the aches and pains and frustrations that we experience now (1 Cor. 15:52–55). Then there is going to be a *summing up* of all things in Christ which we talked about before (Eph. 1:10).

- *Are you ill? In pain? Do bits of you not work as well as they used to? Remembering that you have an incorruptible body to come, do you feel able to praise God in your situation?*
- *Feeling pressurised by the body-conscious, youth-centred culture of today? One day you will have a wonderful new body. How can reflecting on this hope put issues about ageing and looks into perspective?*

Then there is a promise of *reward* for our services. After the description of the resurrection that we are going to experience at the end of chapter 15 of 1 Corinthians, Paul says in verse 58, '. . . be steadfast, immovable, always abounding in the work of the Lord, knowing that in the Lord your labour is not in vain.' There will be a reward. 1 Corinthians 15:19 says if only in this life we have hope in Christ, we are to be pitied more than all men. Yes, there are problems we endure; we have all sorts of crises in our life. And if there was no hope we would be unhappy people, says Paul. What he is saying is that hope is important; it is a basic ingredient of daily living.

- *Make up a 'Christian recipe.' What are other important ingredients, alongside hope, for the Christian life?*
- *Do you know anyone who may have felt they haven't been much of a success in life – at least, not in the world's terms?*

In what ways can reminding them (or ourselves) about the future reward give very real, life-transforming hope?

We all have a sense of justice; we all believe that when someone does something wrong, that person needs to be punished. But it seems as if there is no justice in this life. People hurt us and prosper while we suffer. People are dishonest and become very rich whereas those who are honest don't make so much money. So it seems as though we have a right to be bitter – but not if there's a judgement. If there is a judgement, these things are going to be equalised. There is no need for bitterness over the wicked who prosper. Actually we need to pity them because they are going to face the judgement of God. The doctrine of judgement is a key antidote to bitterness in the present life.

- *Think about someone who has wronged you. Does remembering that there is a judgement affect what you feel about this person?*
- *On a coffee table/flat surface, lay out pictures of people from history such as dictators and those involved in genocide and murderers, terrorists or rapists who have made the news recently. In the middle of the table, place a cross (a wooden one or a necklace or even a cross made from cardboard). Remember that Jesus paid the price for all their sin; God hates the sin but not the sinner. Reflect on these things:*

Jesus didn't just die for 'little' sins or 'acceptable' sins, Jesus took the most heinous sin upon himself on the cross. Because of this, no-one is beyond redemption.

- *What does this tell us of God's love?*
- *What does it tell us about hope?*
- *How does it challenge you as an individual, as well as a group?*

Martin Luther said that 'Everything that is done in the world is done by hope.' That's why we don't break the law though others break it. That's why we don't take revenge when people hurt us. That's why we pay the price of serving other people. That's why we devote ourselves to sharing Christ with all that we can. It's all because we believe in hope; in eternal reward for service. That is not the only reason, but it is a key reason.

So this hope that we are talking about is not 'a pie in the sky by-and-by' which lulls us to indifference amidst injustice. Karl Marx said that religion was the opiate of the masses. This is not true of Christian hope; Christian hope drives us to service. It tells us that paying the price of service is worth it. This is illustrated in the life of John Bunyan who is a great example of the hope of patience. He spent eleven or twelve years in prison for preaching the gospel but while he was in prison he exercised Christian patience, which is active obedience in hope amidst hardship. That's what Christian patience is, it's an active work.

Bunyan had a young wife, his second wife actually. His first wife had died, leaving four children, and the young wife had to look after them. She needed money, so while he was in prison, he stitched stockings and sold them and earned a little money and sent it to his wife. He had a chair with railings, and out of one of the railings he made a flute. He used to play his music when the guard wasn't around. When the guard came to find out where this noise was coming from, he would quickly put back the railing to its normal place. And he wrote several books which resulted in a lot of correspondence being carried out – counselling people, answering questions – while he was in prison. One of the books he wrote was his autobiography, *Grace Abounding to the Chief of Sinners*. It has been called the greatest Puritan spiritual autobiography. All this was done while he was in prison.

Listen to what John Bunyan has to say

Hope has a thick skin and will endure many a blow. It will put on patience as a vestment, it will wade through a sea of blood, it will endure all things if it be of the right kind, for the joy that is set before it. Hence, patience is called "the patience of hope" because it is hope that makes the soul exercise patience and longsuffering under the cross until the time comes to enjoy the crown.

Bunyan was a man who had patience and hope. So hope does not lull us to indifference, it drives us to service.

● *There are many kinds of prisons – including ill-health, fear and bitterness. Are you in some sort of prison today? Talk to God (and the group, if you can) about it.*

C.S. Lewis, in his classic book *Mere Christianity*, points out that those Christians who do most for this world are those who are most concerned about the next: that being just concerned for this world actually renders us ineffective.

So Christians are people with hope. Paul prays that we will realise this hope, we'll understand the hope.

● *A quick quiz: How much are your thoughts centred on this present world (a) never (b) sometimes (c) mostly (d) all the time? Realistically, most of us would answer (c). How might our lives change if we centred our thoughts more wholeheartedly on the world to come?*

● *What does thinking about the next world mean to you? Dreaming about playing a harp? Looking forward to being with Christ for ever? Getting away from everyday problems? Seeing loved ones who have died again? Discuss this in twos, and then brainstorm your answers back to the whole group and add them to the group journal.*

THE INHERITANCE OF THE SAINTS

The next thing we need to know is in the third part of verse 18: 'what are the riches of his glorious inheritance in the saints.' Verse 14 also talked about *our* inheritance. Now Paul talks about God's inheritance in the saints. We are *God's* inheritance.

When I first read this, I assumed Paul was talking about *our* inheritance; the inheritance that God is going to give us. In fact the new Sinhalese Bible, that is the Bible in my language, has it as 'our' inheritance – it's mistranslated. That's what we normally think of when we think of inheritance. But this passage is saying that we are *God's* inheritance; and not just that, we are his *glorious* inheritance.

The Christian pilgrimage begins with accepting our sinfulness and guilt. Some say this is dangerous to our self-esteem. Because society has lost its identity in God and is desperately looking to restore this self-esteem, people are trying to circumvent repentance. They don't know what they are missing. We have a great God who not only forgives us but considers us as his inheritance. Our loss of esteem is overcome more than anything else by this fact.

Our loss of esteem is not only because we are alienated from God, it's also because of the rejection we face on earth – in school, at home, at work, in this competitive world. With so many angry people around, we are going to face rejection. We are going to face the message that says, 'You're useless, you're worthless, you're ugly, you're no good, you're a shame to your family.' So people try to overcome this sense of inadequacy by succeeding in life. Often the commonest measure of success is how wealthy a person is. They think, 'If I can make a lot of money, then I will be a great person.'

Even if they're not wealthy, very often people take on the trappings of wealth because they have credit cards with which they can buy things, so that they can look rich. But the Bible comes with the greater truth to us: you are rich already, because God considers you as his inheritance.

A husband once told his wife, 'One day we will be rich and we'll be able to buy a lot of things.' The wife said, 'We are already rich. Maybe someday we'll have more money and can buy a lot of things.' We are already rich. We are invested with an unbelievable wealth. The one who owns the cattle on a thousand hills, the wealth in every mine, considers us as his inheritance.

● *God considers you as his inheritance. How does this make you feel about yourself and about God?*

In Sri Lanka, in my language, we often call a person 'my treasure' when we want to express affection and how much we appreciate that person. I think for me some of the happiest moments in life are to see my children and my son-in-law doing ministry. My son-in-law is a young preacher. I feel this is my inheritance and I think they also find joy in seeing my joy. And to think that God looks at us like this, as I have said before and says, 'That's my girl. That's my boy' and delights in us. Our greatest wealth is the fact that God loves us and accepts us as his own. Paul realises that people don't sense this naturally. So he prays that they may experience the riches of this.

There's a couple who lived a very wild life before they became Christians. The husband first came to Christ and he became a wonderful Christian. His wife went to church but she wouldn't commit herself fully to Christ. When we asked her why she was not willing to make this commitment, she said, 'I must have my pleasure. I must have pleasure.' Often I used to think, 'How can we reach this person who's looking for pleasure?' and then I thought to myself, 'She's a pleasure-seeker and I am a pleasure-seeker also but I have found that the great pleasure that I have is in the love of Christ. And not only does that give me pleasure, it gives me a great wealth.' This lady did finally commit her life to Christ.

● *'If I become a Christian I won't be able to sleep with my girlfriend – I don't want to give up sex.' 'I'll become a Christian just before I die. That way I can do what I like and get heaven too.' 'Christianity? That's not for me. I could never be that good all the time.' What would you say to these people?*

● *Tempted to envy 'worldly' people? Read Psalm 73.*

We are rich people. There was a tax assessor who came to a poor home and asked the husband there to list his possessions. And the husband said, 'First, I have everlasting life. Second, I have a mansion in heaven. Third, I have peace that passes all understanding. Fourth, I have joy unspeakable. Fifth, I have divine love which never fails. Sixth, I have a faithful wife. Seventh, I have healthy, happy, obedient children. Eighth, I have loyal friends. Ninth, I have songs in the night. Tenth, I have a crown of life.' And the tax assessor closed his book and said, 'Truly you are a very rich man. But your property is not subject to taxation.' We are rich people because of the glory of the gospel.

FURTHER STUDY

Read Hebrews chapter 11. It starts off: 'Now faith is being sure of what we hope for and certain of what we do not see' (NIV). As you read, think about the importance of hope for Christians who are 'aliens and strangers on earth.'

REFLECTION AND RESPONSE

• How can you keep in mind the hope of the wonderful future you have in Christ and the meaning of real riches, as you go about your daily business this week? You may decide to read Revelation 21 and 22 in your Quiet Time; write 'Hope of glory', 'I'm rich' or 'Remember the future' on a beautiful picture/photo/decorated card and place it where you will often notice it. You could caption a photograph of yourself as 'God's inheritance' and use as a screensaver.

• Do you know anyone who is resisting the gospel because they prefer to have a life of worldly pleasure? Pray for them.

• Add a reference to Psalm 73 to the group journal, or get someone to write it out fully in beautiful hand-writing and add any comments or prayers about hope and the meaning of true wealth.

CHAPTER 14

Resurrection power

Aim: To grasp the fact that resurrection power is available to us

FOCUS ON THE THEME
Think about a specific time when God has intervened in your life, perhaps when a positive outcome seemed impossible. How did that time build your faith? Share with the group. If you can't think of an example from your own life, perhaps you have read or heard another testimony you can share.

Read: Ephesians 1:18–23
Key verses: Ephesians 1:19,20

Having talked about the hope of our calling and the inheritance of the saints, Paul turns to the superlative resurrection power. Verse 19, 'and what is the immeasurable greatness of his power toward us who believe, according to the working of his great might that he worked in Christ when he raised him from the dead and seated him at his right hand in the heavenly places . . .' He's talking about the immeasurable greatness of his power.

THE CROSS BEFORE POWER

Look at how Paul, in the next few verses, piles words on words to make a great impact. Look at this – 'immeasurable greatness of his power.' Then, 'according to the working of his great might' – 'according to the working of the might of his strength' – working, might, strength: they say almost the same thing. He's piling word upon word to tell us how powerful a thing this is. Peter O'Brien says that 'Paul has piled up equivalents because he wants to convince his readers that God's power, working on behalf of believers, is incomparable.'

I was studying this at a very bad time. It was a week before I left on this journey. I needed a visa. I was coming to the UK with a colleague of mine and the two of us needed visas to pass through Amsterdam airport. I thought a week would do for the visa, so I went to the Netherlands embassy with my colleague. But when we went, we were told that we would have to phone for an interview, that they couldn't accept our applications; and then, after that, it'd take four days to process the visa.

I came home and phoned. The earliest time for an interview was a week later, eight hours after I was scheduled to leave the country. I was really upset. I called my travel agent. I said, 'I don't know what to do. Please try and do something.'

I had a little free time before my next appointment, so I took my wife to buy a gift for a boy in our church. While she was buying the gift, I was studying Ephesians in the van. I read about God's incomparable power for believers. My first reaction was, 'This is not true for Sri Lankans. We are so weak and helpless. I'm tired of international travel. I'm treated like a fraud until I'm proven innocent. This is too stressful, too humiliating, this whole process of getting visas. And . . . and now my wife is getting late.' I had another appointment and she wasn't coming. She had wanted to buy a book for a child whose father had left them and all the books that she saw in the book shop talked about a father's love. Finally, she got a drawing book but because she was getting late, I had more time to reflect on this verse.

Suddenly a thought came to me. 'This is the power of resurrection and exaltation.' Before resurrection, there is crucifixion. This supreme Christ, who's giving us this power, went through humiliation, shame, frustration and deep, deep pain. He experienced more suffering than any other human had ever experienced, because the Sinless one became sin, which is the greatest of all the suffering that Jesus endured on the cross.

I began to write down 'My Master didn't avoid the cross before triumph. How could I?' The joy of dying and rising is greater than the joy of those who didn't need such death. In fact, many people today who don't have problems are bored with life; everything is so easy for them. Easter would be nothing if Good Friday were not so painful. Tony Campolo used to tell the story of a person who would say, 'It's Friday but Sunday's coming.'

● *'Easter would be nothing if Good Friday were not so painful.' Do you agree?*

I came home with a word from the Lord and found that my son had got on his bicycle and was looking for me, because there was an urgent message asking me to call the travel agent. KLM had appealed on my behalf and I was asked to call the embassy again. I had an interview the next morning. I went twenty minutes late for my next appointment but I went very happy because God had intervened.

We have heroes in Christianity – heroes because they served faithfully despite the huge problems. They had experienced resurrection power. There is no resurrection power if it is not preceded by a cross. We think of the first martyrs of the church, Stephen and James. But today I was thinking of the families of Stephen and James. They had to go through a life of hardship. Stephen and James went to heaven but their families had to go through life with a void because their loved one had gone. But Jesus was there with resurrection power.

I thought of Paul. He faced so many attacks, so much pain, so much loneliness but he pressed on, believing in God. I thought of Steve Brady this morning, as I was preparing this, who is bravely serving God with so much joy. Steve exudes joy and his wife is suffering from multiple sclerosis.

I thought of Adoniram Judson, the great missionary to Myanmar. He spent seventeen months in prison. Two of his wives died. Two children died. But he was a great translator. There were seven years of service before the first converts were baptised. Now there's a large church there.

There's no resurrection power without first going through the cross.

● *How has thinking about God's resurrection power coming after the experience of the cross spoken to you as individuals and as a group? What encouragement does this thought bring to those who are going through 'the cross' experience today? Is there anyone you can encourage with the thought of resurrection power by phoning, emailing or visiting this week?*

THE EXALTATION OF CHRIST

Paul talks about the power of resurrection and exaltation that God worked, in verse 20, in Christ 'when he raised him from the dead and seated him at his right hand in the heavenly places . . . ' In Philippians 3:10, Paul says he wants to know 'the power of his resurrection.' Here he wants to know the power that God worked in Christ when he raised him from the dead and seated him at his right hand in the heavenly places.

In Paul's writings, the resurrection and exaltation are mentioned together – all as part of the exaltation of Christ. Murray Harris has written a book on the resurrection which he called *From Grave to Glory*[23] – highlighting this point. You see this in Peter's talk at Pentecost. You see it in Paul's great hymn in Philippians 2. Exaltation is an event that we must not forget. I think we don't usually preach on the ascension. Ascension Sunday is a good time for us to remind our people of the greatness of Christ's exaltation.

See how that exaltation is mentioned. Jesus is seated at the right hand. That means that his work is complete, that's why he's seated. But also to be seated at someone's right hand is to be in a position of special honour and privilege. It means sharing the Father's throne. Chapter 2 and verse 6 says that we, the believers, are raised up and are seated with Christ in heavenly places. But we are not seated at the right hand of God.

Murray Harris says, 'Angels stand or fall in worship (1 Kgs. 22:19; Rev. 4:10). In God's presence, the Exalted One sits.' Jesus is exalted, and a great power was exercised in raising him from the dead and exalting him. And Paul says that power is now available for us.

What does this mean? It means, firstly, that resurrection and exaltation completed the work of Christ so that we can experience the benefits of his work. Our foes are defeated. The door to salvation is now open. Our part is to believe, as this passage says. So the work is complete because of resurrection and exaltation. Secondly, it is the resurrection that gives us strength to believe that God's power is available. If God could raise up Christ like this from the dead, then surely he can help us. Resurrection helps us to believe and belief unleashes resurrection power. It helps us to believe and when we believe, resurrection power is unleashed in our life.

● *Look at the resurrection from a fresh perspective by imagining yourself as Peter, Thomas, John or Mary Magdalene. In twos, relate how 'you' felt when you saw Jesus for the first time after his resurrection. Afterwards, ask: how has this exercise helped to build up your faith?*

One of the most helpful verses in the Bible for the Christian, for Christian living, is Romans 8:32: 'He who did not spare his own Son but gave him up for us all – how will he not also, along with him, graciously give us all things?' We have everything that we need because God loved us. And how do we know God loves us? He did not spare his only Son.

There's a difference between the love of God and the love of a mother. Take a situation where a mother is willing to die for her child, just like Jesus. The father comes home drunk and goes to hit the child and the mother comes in between, willing to die for the sake of that child. But what does the father do? He brushes aside that mother and goes and hits that child. Why? She has love but she doesn't have power. God not only has love enough to die for us, that love was backed by a power that was powerful enough to raise Jesus from the dead. This is the greatest power possible.

● *How does it make you want to respond to your Creator, knowing that God loves us and can back that love up with power?*

If we believe, we can have this power – if we don't believe, we close the door to power; we develop attitudes which prevent God from acting so that we won't have this power.

● *Have you developed attitudes that have closed the door to God's power? What might they be? If you can think of any, write them down.*

I was writing on this verse in the Dutch embassy the next day, while I was waiting for my interview. I wrote 'What are the things that prevent us from experiencing this power?' The first thing I wrote down was 'We fret.' We get anxious and we fret. Then I thought to myself, '*I* get anxious and fret. I fretted a lot, especially when I heard about this interview.' Then I said, 'But still God seems to be giving me some sort of experience of his power.' I asked, 'How? How can we have experience of power, if we fret?' Well, inside of us, in the midst of all the fretting – the fretting is our natural response – there is a mustard seed-sized faith, a faith that deep down says, 'God will look after me.' That faith addresses the heart and says, 'Leave it in God's hands. You do what God wants you to do and God will do the rest.'

So, to get out of the tough situation, we won't lie, we won't bribe, we won't take revenge, we won't slander, we won't use violence or force, we won't give up and say, 'It doesn't work.' If we do that, we will forfeit the blessing. Our natural reaction is to fret. But when the natural reaction has been expressed – hopefully not very publicly – soon faith acts on it and helps us to be obedient. And as we are obedient, God's power is unleashed. That's why Jesus said, if you have faith as small as a mustard seed, you can do great things for him.

● *Take the anxiety test. What do you find yourself fretting over the most*
    – *Your health/someone else's health*
    – *Money*
    – *Relationships*
    – *The future*
    – *Your job*
    – *Your children/grandchildren*
    – *Other*

Our impossibilities are God's opportunities. Do you need to take any steps to obey God so that his power can be unleashed in your situation?

● *Are any of these examples tied in with the attitudes you wrote down earlier that might have closed the door to God's power in your life? You may like to pray with someone about this.*

THE HOLY SPIRIT

There's another sense in which resurrection power comes to us and that is because the exaltation made it possible for the Holy Spirit to come down to this world. John 16:7 says, 'it is to your advantage that I go away, for if I do not go away the Helper will not come to you; but if I go, I will send him to you.' As I was going through this passage, I was thinking of Mary, the mother of Jesus. How sad she must have been. Her Son, in the prime of his life, was taken away and here she was with a hole in her heart because her Son was gone. But Jesus says, 'It's better that I go,' because when he goes, the Holy Spirit is going to come back.

Many of us have faced sorrow and pain as loved ones have gone. That pain will be there until we die, but along with the pain there is the love of a God who comes and lives with us and gives us strength to live the Christian life. So we are better off.

● *Are you grieving? Do you know someone who is? Pray that you (or they) will know the strength and power of God today.*

The Holy Spirit comes with resurrection power. He gives us the new birth (Jn. 3:5–8), he guides us (Rom. 8:14); he helps us to be holy by giving us the ability to put to death the deeds of the body (Rom. 8:13); he gives us peace and joy (Rom. 14:17); he gives us an abundance of love (Rom. 5:5); he helps us to pray when we don't know how to pray (Rom. 8:26); he gives us power to witness (Acts 1:8) and he gives unity among Christians in the bond of peace (Eph. 4:3). So whatever crisis we face, we have resurrection power through the indwelling Holy Spirit. Resurrection power turned the greatest tragedy into the greatest triumph, so whatever we face, we also can today be 'more than conquerors through him who loved us' (Rom. 8:37).

This power helps us to believe and because it helps us to believe, it helps us to obey. The basis of power in chapters 1 to 3 sets the stage for the exhortation of chapters 4 to 6, according to Peter O'Brien, because of all that God has done. We can believe that God will see us through but chapters 4 to 6 still present some great challenges to us. They talk about maintaining the bond of peace within the church and we know how difficult that is. Christians are not the easiest people to live with! Yet there is a resurrection power for this. It talks about giving up past sins and putting on holiness; we know that that is difficult. It talks about battling with spiritual forces; that is difficult. But resurrection power is there for us.

When I go back home, a person that I have been working with for many years, who has been in and out of drugs, will have come out from a centre so I will meet him a day or two after I return. I have almost given up hope – he comes and he goes. But when I go and see him in a few days' time, I have to tell him, 'God can help you' because that's what the Bible says. There is nothing that God cannot do to give us a victorious life. We believe there is hope because God's power is greater and is available to us.

● *Meditate on these facts: God raised Jesus from the dead;
Christ is exalted; the Holy Spirit is here. God has supplied
power for you to live a victorious Christian life. Are you
living in that power today?*

FURTHER STUDY
We have already looked at some of the work of the Holy Spirit
during further study in chapter 9. Now, read John 3:5–8; Acts 1:8;
Acts 2:1–18; Romans 8:1–27; Ephesians 4:3. How do these verses
inspire, stimulate, encourage and challenge you?

REFLECTION AND RESPONSE
• Write down the three headings from this chapter: The cross before
power, the exaltation of Christ, the power of the Holy Spirit. Split
the group into three and take a heading each. Make notes about
all you have learned and then come back to share everything as a
group.

• Spend time quietly asking the Holy Spirit to come and refresh your
hearts and minds and to fall in power upon each of you this week.

• Finish by singing or playing a song about the exaltation of Christ.

CHAPTER 15

The supremacy of Christ

Aim: To understand that Christ is above all, for the church

FOCUS ON THE THEME
Think of a well-known Bible story about someone who has been in a situation from which they had no power to escape . . . but God delivered them, e.g. Peter in prison, Daniel in the lions' den or (more adventurously) the story of Joseph, sold into slavery but ending up in a position of authority. Get into teams and tell the story you have chosen in as few words as possible. The team that uses the fewest words to tell a recognisable version of the story wins.

Read: Ephesians 1:18–23
Key verses: Ephesians 1:21–23

CHRIST ABOVE ALL

Along with the exaltation of Christ, something else takes place. Christ triumphs over other powers. Verse 21 says '. . . far above all rule and authority, power and dominion and above every name that is named, not only in this age but also in the one to come.' Higher than other forces . . . In verse 19, Paul piled expression upon expression to bring the idea of the power of God, now he's doing the same thing to bring the idea of the superiority of Christ over other authorities.

In Paul's ministry in Ephesus there was a lot of confrontation with supernatural forces. The battle would go on. Therefore in Ephesians, Paul talks about power more than in any other book. In verse 20 he says that Christ is seated in heavenly places. This is where principalities and powers operate and we wrestle against these, says Paul (Eph. 6:12); but this is where Christ is also. The only difference is he is placed far above all this rule and authority and power and dominion.

That's not all. He is above every name that is named. When 'name' is used in this way, it's talking about possessing authority. The NIV translates it as 'every title', which is a good expression: though the word is 'name,' it carries the idea of title.

People who think that they possess authority are under Jesus. I was still in the Dutch embassy when I was studying this verse. My colleague had gone for his interview and it would be my time in a short while. My colleague had been refused once before to go to Amsterdam for a conference for evangelists. 'Will he make it, will he not?' I knew I would make it because I travel there quite often. I was nervous and afraid about my colleague. Then I remembered, I shouldn't be afraid of these authorities because nothing can thwart God's plans; Christ is above these authorities. If Christ wants us to go, he will open the door. And he did!

● *Is there a situation in your own life where you need to know that nothing can thwart God's plan?*

A few days ago, anti-conversion legislation passed the committee stage in our Parliament. Now it's ready to be presented for debate and voting. This process has taken several years. It has had several hiccups along the way but now it's finally going to be presented and the maximum sentence for unethical conversion – for conversion through inducements – is seven years. And the law is particularly harsh on evangelism among children, young people, people in hospitals, in rehabilitation camps and soldiers. I work for a youth organisation. My daughter works for a children's ministry. What shall we do when this happens? We work with people who are outside the church, not with Christians. What are we going to do? Shall we stop evangelism and work with Christian youth? Or train people in youth evangelism without doing evangelism ourselves?

We need to be alert to the situation. We need to be very wise but we cannot disobey God or move away from our call. Some people may suffer but the witness of history is that times of persecution are a springboard to great growth of the church. This is what happened in China, in Uganda and in Korea. That's what we've been praying for all these years in our country and all we have seen has been mercy drops, no showers yet. God has allowed this repressive legislation to come so far . . . we are going to pray that it won't pass but if God wishes for it to pass, it's because he has some greater plan. He's above these authorities; we don't need to be afraid.

It looks like the Ephesians were getting afraid of the powers that they had been under earlier, and these powers hit us too. Very often you find that when Christians fall into serious sin, it's the same sins that they committed before they were converted. Later Satan hits us, and we wonder, can we make it? And some have sadly succumbed. But they don't need to. Christ is above these forces. He'll give us victory if we let him.

● *Sometimes we can't believe God could allow certain things to happen but they do. Seeing these things as something God has permitted challenges our faith. Is your faith being tested at the moment?*

● *Is there something 'wrong' in your life that stems from your pre-Christian days? It might be a sexual sin or something like smoking, swearing, gossip etc. Spend a few moments being real with God about your struggle; share with the group if you feel you can. Remember that Christ is above the enemy's forces. How does that make you feel?*

Verse 22 says that Christ is not only above these forces, it says that God has put all things under his feet and given him as Head over all things to the church. Not only is he above them, he has subjected them – they are under his feet. Now he is their Head. These forces cannot do anything without God's permission. Terrible things happen to Christians, true. But these powers cannot go beyond what God has permitted. What now looks like a huge blow will one day emerge as the key to a great victory.

FOR THE CHURCH

Paul finally comes to a climax. God 'put all things under his feet and gave him as head over all things *to the church*' (v22). All of this is for the benefit of the church. Christ is absolute Lord of the universe. He's head of all things and has been given to the church.

William Barclay says that in these two verses, 22 and 23, Paul has one of the most adventurous and uplifting thoughts that man has ever had. Jesus is given to the church, in other words, for her advantage, for her benefit. This great Lord who is above everything is also our Shepherd, our Provider, our Protector, our Guard, our Guide, our Friend, our Comforter, our Counsellor. He's not only Lord, he's *our* Lord. Wonderful things have been said about Christ and his glory. Right at the climax, Paul says, 'He's for you – his greatness is directed towards you.'

● *Think again of difficult circumstances in your own life or in*
the church or world. Does seeing Christ as given to the
church for our benefit encourage you? Praise him for who he
is and what he has done – and for what he is going to do.

Paul says all this is for the church and then describes the
church: '. . . which is his body, the fullness of him who fills all
in all' (v23). The blessings of God are not given just to
individuals. True, the blessing *is* given to individuals but the
context in which it is given to individuals is the church. You
never think – 'My finger has been given a wonderful blessing.
A nice ring has come to my finger.' No. I have got this ring,
even though the finger is the part that carries the ring. It's like
that with us. When God blesses us, he's blessing the church.

This is one of the weakest points of evangelical
Christianity. God used the evangelical movement to bring
back the importance of personal decision – of what it means
to personally come to Christ, to be born again. But in the
process many of us forgot that we are born again into a
body; we are part of a body. John Wesley says, 'The Bible
knows nothing of solitary religion.' When we pray for
something, we are not praying only for ourselves. That
thing is for the whole church.

● *There can be many reasons why some Christians choose to*
'go it alone.' They might have been very hurt in the past by
Christians and the church. Think of ways you can encourage
them to join in with the life of the church, to feel important
to the body, wanted and loved. Do you find yourself judging
them instead of trying to include them?

● *Are you tempted to solitary discipleship? Has this study*
encouraged you to become more involved in the church?
Would it be appropriate for you to speak to someone about
any past hurts or failings within Christ's body, things that
have alienated you?

I have a regular time of prayer with our accounts staff and one of them is a twin. We ask for their personal requests and the twin almost always says, 'Pray that *we* will have this; pray this for *us*.' She has learned to look at life along with her twin sister. It's the same with us. Our needs are the church's needs. Our blessings are the church's blessings. And so, if your daughter sits for her exams and she gets two As and maybe some Bs whereas the daughter of another member of your church gets ten As, you don't get angry and fret and get all upset. You say, 'Thank you Lord. I got ten As because part of my body has got those ten As.' We rejoice together; the church is Christ's body, so that we do it all together.

● *When do we as Christians feel able to rejoice together? When is it more difficult? Why?*

Then he says, '. . . who fills all in all.' There is a little confusion as to what is meant by Christ filling the body; Christ filling 'all in all.' Some think it is that we fill up Christ in the sense that we are the bride and when the bride is united with the Bridegroom then the Bridegroom is filled up. I think a more probable meaning is that Christ fills the church. John Stott puts it like this: 'As the head of the body, Christ directs it. As the fullness of the body, he fills it and completes it.'

SUMMARY

Let's summarise what we have been learning. Christ is Lord of all; the fullness of Christ is available to the church and the implication is that no force can thwart Christ's plans for the church, so we have no reason to fear. The only thing we have to fear is disobedience because that will hinder God from working in our lives.

So as a conclusion, let me say that Ephesians 1 has talked about the riches that we have in Christ. We are rich people but we have to possess our possessions. In a parallel passage, Paul says, 'I want to know him and the power of his resurrection and the fellowship of sharing in his suffering so that I may attain the resurrection of the dead' (Phil. 3:10,11). Then in the next verse he says, 'But I press on to lay hold of that for which I was laid hold of by Christ Jesus.' What he is saying is, 'God laid hold of me for a purpose. Now I must lay hold of that purpose for which I was laid hold of. God grasped me for something; now I must grasp that.'

There was a young preacher who said, after some years in ministry, 'I've been perjuring myself. I've been preaching things that are not operative in me. I'm through with this unreality. I'll give God till Sunday to do something for me. If he doesn't do something for me before Sunday, someone else can preach. I won't preach.' So he took Saturday off as a day of retreat and he spent the time with God, saying, 'Oh God, help me to experience you. Give me your fullness.' The Lord met him on that Saturday. On Sunday he went to church to preach and the congregation got the shock of their lives. It seemed as if they had a new minister. Here was a man who had been filled by God. And the congregation found themselves seeking what the young minister had found.

You remember the revival that took place in the Hebrides Islands in Scotland? There were two places where great prayer was taking place. One was two ladies who were praying for revival in their church. The other was a group of leaders in a church who said that they were using a passage from Isaiah, that they would give God no rest until he sent revival to their town. And so they began to pray. And they prayed for some time and one day when they were on their knees, one of the brothers got up and read Psalm 24, verses 3 and 4, which says 'Who shall ascend the hill of the Lord?

Who shall stand in his holy place? He who has clean hands and a pure heart.' He said, 'This is all humbug, praying like this week after week. We have to ask ourselves, do we have clean hands and a pure heart?' And that day God met them as they repented before God and God filled them and the fullness went through the whole islands. Hundreds of people were ushered into the kingdom.

I pray that as you leave this place, you will leave saying, 'Oh God, I want to be filled by you. I want to possess my possessions. I want to go, not as a poor person but as a wealthy person, filled with the love of God.' Let's pray that God will do that to us.

● *Can you pray the prayer above and mean it? If you can, do it now. And be prepared for God to do something amazing in your life.*

FURTHER STUDY

We have learned a great deal just by studying the first chapter of Ephesians. You may like to study in depth the rest of the book, with the group, perhaps using a good concordance or another study book. You might also like to read Watchman Nee's insightful *Sit, Walk, Stand*, teaching from the book of Ephesians.[24] You may wish to pick out themes from this study and see how they recur in Paul's other writings and the book of Hebrews.

REFLECTION AND RESPONSE

• Reflect for a while on the facts that God's plans cannot be thwarted and that Christ is head over all – for the church.

• In twos, spend some time praying together for any situation known to you where people need to see that Jesus is Lord; pray for difficult situations within the worldwide church; that your church as well as individuals within the body clearly know and respond to what God is calling you to 'grasp'; and that your church leadership/congregation be filled with the fullness of God. You may also like to pray for the Group Project (missionary/ organisation) and note anything that has personally challenged you in the group journal.

- Remember that Jesus is Lord of all this week; no plan of his can be thwarted and he is in charge. Worship him as Lord of every situation in your Quiet Times, by song or in prayer; by creative words, dance, mime, drawing/painting; or more practically, by contacting or visiting the lonely or alienated or by encouraging someone to 'go for it', whatever God is calling them to do.

- Finish by saying this prayer all together.

  Father, you have done such extraordinary things. Save us from being ordinary. Come, Lord, and fill us with yourself, that we might be wealthy people and out of our wealth may streams of healing flow into our community and into our land. Oh God, we pray, send revival upon (name your town) and may it begin with us being revived, with us possessing our possessions. Give us that earnest desire that will not rest until you have filled us, that we will give you no rest until we have sensed that we have experienced what you want us to experience. Oh God, we pray that you will fill us with yourself and we ask these things in Jesus' name. Amen.

REVIEW OF EPHESIANS 1:18–23:
We have learned about the hope of our calling, the inheritance of the saints, resurrection power and that the cross comes before it; the exaltation of Christ, the Holy Spirit. We have also seen that Jesus is supreme; he is above all for the church. Write down anything that has especially challenged you and read out to the group.

- Review everything you have noted in the group journal. Has the theology you've studied changed your practical Christianity? Share examples.

• If you were writing a letter to some friends, as Paul wrote to the Ephesians, how might you encourage them with what you have learned from the first chapter of Ephesians?

POINTS TO PONDER

• What have you learned about God?

• What have you learned about yourself?

• What actions or attitudes do you need to change as a result?

ENDNOTES

1   R. Kent Hughes, *Ephesians: the mystery of the Body of Christ* (Leicester: Crossway books, 1990)

2   Lindsay Brown, *Shining like stars: the power of the gospel in the world's universities* (Leicester: IVP, 2006)

3   Harry Blamires, *The Christian Mind: how should a Christian think?* (Vancouver: Regents College publishing: 2005)

4   Peter T. O'Brien, *The letter to the Ephesians – Pillar New Testament commentary* (Grand Rapids: W B Eerdmans, 1999)

5   Eusebius, *The church history of Eusebius, The Nicene and post-Nicene Fathers, Second series, Volume 1* (Electronic version by AGES Software, 1997)

6   Tertullian, *On baptism, The Ante-Nicene Fathers Volume 3* (Electronic version by AGES Software, 1997)

7   Stanley Porter, (ed.), *Exegesis of Pauline letters, including the Deutero-Pauline letters in Handbook to Exegesis of the New Testament* (Leiden: Brill, 1997) p533

8   James S. Stewart, *A man in Christ* (Vancouver: Regents College publishing, 2002)

9   Bruce Narramore, *Freedom from guilt* (Caroline House publications, 1976)

10 Sam Gordon, *The genius of grace: the message of Ephesians: Truth for today series* (Greenville SC: Ambassador-Emerald International, 2003)

11 J.I. Packer, *Knowing God* (London: Hodder & Stoughton, 2005)

12 Stibbs was an Englishman and Leon Morris was an Australian. In the mid-twentieth century, they wrote two very important books that were very influential in developing evangelical theology that was credible in the early years of the revival of intellectual evangelical scholarship

[13] Leon Morris, *The atonement* (Downers Grove: IVP, 1983), p129

[14] Gustaf Aulen, *Christus Victor: an historical study of the three main types of the idea of atonement* (Eugene, Or: Wipf and Stock, 2003)

[15] Rabindranath R. Majaraj with Dave Hunt, *Death of a Guru* (London: Hodder & Stoughton, 1986) p203

[16] Rudolf Bultmann, *Kerygma and myth* (London: SPCK, 1962) p7

[17] Lindsay Brown, *Shining like stars: the power of the gospel in the world's universities* (Leicester: IVP, 2006)

[18] Fanny Crosby, 1820-1915. This material has been taken from Jane Stuart-Smith and Betty Carson, *Great Christian hymnwriters* (Wheaton: Crossway books, 1977), pp59-64

[19] Dietrich Bonhoeffer in *The martyred Christian*, compiled by Joan Winmill Brown (New York: Macmillan Publishing Co., 1983) p91f

[20] Rodney Stark, *The rise of Christianity* (HarperSanFrancisco, 1997)

[21] Robert Coleman, *The mind of the Master* (Fleming H. Revell, 1989)

[22] Martin Luther, *Table talk: Luther's comments on life, the church and the Bible* (Ross-shire: Christian Focus publications, 2003)

[23] Murray J. Harris, *From grave to glory: resurrection in the New Testament* (Zondervan, 1990)

[24] Watchman Nee, *The normal Christian life – incorporating Sit, walk, stand* (Eastbourne: Kingsway, 2005)